100 Ideas for
Primary Teachers

Computing

Steve Bunce

B L O O M S B U R Y
LONDON • OXFORD • NEW YORK • NEW DELHI • SYDNEY

Bloomsbury Education
An imprint of Bloomsbury Publishing Plc

50 Bedford Square
London
WC1B 3DP
UK

1385 Broadway
New York
NY 10018
USA

www.bloomsbury.com

Bloomsbury is a registered trade mark of Bloomsbury Publishing Plc

First published 2015

© Steve Bunce, 2015

British Library Cataloguing-in-Publication Data
A catalogue record for this book is available from the British Library.

ISBN: PB: 9781472914996
ePub: 9781472915009
ePDF: 9781472915016

Library of Congress Cataloging-in-Publication Data
A catalog record for this book is available from the Library of Congress.

10 9 8 7 6 5 4 3 2 1

Typeset by Newgen Knowledge Works (P) Ltd., Chennai, India
Printed by CPI Group (UK) Ltd, Croydon, CR0 4YY

This book is produced using paper that is made from wood grown
in managed, sustainable forests. It is natural, renewable and
recyclable. The logging and manufacturing processes conform
to the environmental regulations of the country of origin.

To view more of our titles please visit www.bloomsbury.com

Contents

Acknowledgements

Many people have shared and inspired teachers to learn more about computing. The Computing at School community has developed resources for progression and to develop Computational Thinking, so thanks go to Mark Dorling (@MarkDorling) and Simon Humphreys (@simonHumph) and Miles Berry (@mberry). Thanks go to Mark Clarkson (@mwclarkson), Zoe Ross (@zoeross19), Paul Hutton (@krowdrah) and Simon Finch (@simfin) for sharing enthusiasm and practical ideas.

At Bloomsbury, many thanks to Holly Gardner for her work in guiding, editing and producing this book.

Most of all, my precious family have been so supportive. They have encouraged me to put these ideas together and they have been willing testers too!

Thank you, Anna, Verity, Josie and Will.

Thank you Mum and Dad.

Introduction

Computing, and especially programming, for children is often mentioned in the news. Many people are keen to 'get kids coding' as they see it could be beneficial for children in their careers and also for the economy of the nation. The NESTA Next Gen report in 2011 (www.nesta.org.uk/publications/next-gen) highlighted the need for action to develop the next generation of creative media and video games programmers.

Some teachers can remember their experiences of programming through the BBC Micro Model B programme, which introduced schools to the BASIC programming language. Home computers, which could be programmed, were developed from the 1980s onwards, such as the ZX81, ZX Spectrum, Commodore 64 and Amiga. Following this, video games developed on consoles and computers, with some games offering the ability to create levels. More recently, games like 'Little Big Planet' on the Playstation 3 allow level creation and sharing. The XBOX 360 console can be used with KODU, game creation software (available for PC), which enables games to be created, using its visual game commands.

In primary schools, the ICT curriculum has included the use of Scratch from MIT Media Lab. This has enabled children to create simple programs and animations, using the LOGO-based programming blocks, which fit together like jigsaw pieces. When used, a strong context for learning really helps the children to develop their programming.

The introduction of the iPad into schools has brought classroom access to many apps, which can be used to teach computing. There are some apps which have been organised under the 'Education' section of the Apple App Store, which can help teachers and parents find ones suitable for use in schools or with children. However, there are many other games, such as Angry Birds, Amazing Alex or the LEGO games, which can teach children about number, problem solving and many computational thinking concepts.

With the introduction of the National Curriculum for computing in September 2014, there is a new emphasis on computing in education. To support teachers new to this subject, this book contains 100 practical and accessible ideas to inspire the children. Computing can be taught across many subjects, reinforcing the learning.

Please try out the ideas and feed back your experiences on social media using #100ideas. As I often say at the start of a lesson, 'What could possibly go wrong?' The children can learn by making mistakes and collaborating to try again. That is where I have learned the most from them.

The book is organised into ten sections:

1. What is computing? – an introduction to computing and computational thinking
2. Algorithms, instructions and recipes – solving problems using little steps
3. The computer says 'Yes' – programming ideas – developing programming using different tools and software
4. Searching – finding out information, by using the web
5. Staying safe – e-safety and thinking about being safe online
6. How do computers work? – ideas for learning about the way computers work and communicate with each other
7. Data, data, data – ideas for looking at how data is becoming more part of our lives and how it can move from one place to another
8. Technology around us – we are surrounded by technology, can we spot it and work out what it is doing?
9. Progression – thinking about how the children can progress and how we can observe it
10. Assessment – ideas for assessing the children's activities

How to use this book

Whether you are an experienced computing teacher or new to the subject, this book aims to share practical ideas to use in the classroom. By using examples taken from across the curriculum, it shows how many aspects of computing are included in everyday life.

Each idea includes:

- A short title to engage the children and your teaching colleagues.
- An opening quote to provide further context, a quote from the National Curriculum for computing or from the Computing at Schools (CAS) advice.
- A summary in bold to help explain the big picture behind the idea.
- A short description of how to try out the idea in your school, which can be adapted for your children.

In addition to the main idea, extra advice or guidance can be found with:

Teaching tip

The teaching tip comes from experience of trying the ideas in the classroom. It gives extra advice and prompts your thoughts on how the idea may run with your children.

Taking it further

This explains how the idea could be differentiated or extended to provide next steps. It is important to think about how each one could be adapted for the children and to move their learning forward.

Bonus idea ★

This is an extra idea, which could be added to the main idea. It could be another example, based on the theme of the main idea.

Tablet tip

Where schools have access to tablet computers, there are many ways that they can help to teach computing. There are many apps, some for teaching coding and others which can be used to teach computing concepts. The Tablet tip can mention an app or idea to use.

What is computing?   Part 1

What is computational thinking?

"DON'T PANIC!"

Computing is an exciting subject, but many of the words used can put people off. In reality, many parts of computing are being taught already. Let's have a look!

At the heart of the new computing curriculum is 'computational thinking'. This is a range of approaches, which embrace the power of critical thinking and computers. A useful video by the International Society for Technology in Education (ISTE) shows how technology can help us and how we need to teach computational thinking to our children to help them to solve problems and harness the power of computing (vimeo.com/49000273).

How do we define computational thinking? The Computing at School organisation has prepared a useful document to help us better understand it (bit.ly/100computing1b). They break it down into five main areas: algorithmic thinking; evaluation; decomposition; abstraction; generalisation. In the following ideas, I will explain these areas and why they will help our children to become successful problem solvers.

So, let's try to think of a definition of computational thinking and send it to ourselves . . . in the future! Using a tool called 'Futureme' (www.futureme.org), we can send an email to be delivered at a future date. Why not write a simple definition of computational thinking after looking at the video from ISTE. Set a date in a month's time. Will you still agree with yourself?

Understanding algorithms

"Oh, to understand what algorithms are."

What is an algorithm? Where do we find them? Are they important?

When the draft National Curriculum for computing was released, many teachers were daunted by the vocabulary. I was often asked, what is an algorithm?

We use algorithms every day for instructions, for example, getting dressed, eating breakfast, travelling to school. An algorithm is a series of steps to follow, which help to solve a problem. A recipe has clear instructions including the ingredients, the quantities and the techniques. The chef follows each step to cook the food. What is important is to be precise. The more precise the instructions, the more accurately they will be carried out.

It is really important that the children recognise algorithms as everyday instructions. Use the word 'algorithm' and keep reinforcing the definition. Try the following ideas:

- Playing simple games is a great way of sharing the rules or instructions to play. Play 'Simon says' with the children; they know that when you say 'Simon says' they need to follow the instruction precisely.
- Board games, such as Chess, Monopoly and Cluedo, all have instructions. Ask the children to choose a game they enjoy playing (a board game or sport). Challenge them to explain how to play the game in ten rules or instructions.
- Emphasise to the children that algorithms need to be precise. As humans we can infer what an instruction may mean but computers follow the instructions exactly, so they need more accurate steps to perform correctly.

Teaching tip

Ask the children to write their instructions for a game on a mini whiteboard or on a computer, leaving at least one line in-between each one. That way, they can easily add an intermediate step, to make the instructions even more precise and accurate.

Tablet tip

Using the camera on a tablet computer, ask the children to video themselves playing the game. They could then play it back to identify the rules. They could even edit the video, into short clips, to demonstrate the rules.

Evaluation is key

"How did we do?"

Once children have created a solution to a problem, they need to be able to evaluate how well they have done it. They need to develop a vocabulary for evaluating their work.

Evaluation is very important. When children create a program, they should evaluate it to see if it solves the problem. However, they need help to form the right sort of questions to ask, for example:

- Does it solve the problem faster? (Quicker)
- Does it solve the problem more accurately? (Precise)
- Does it solve the problem more reliably? (Fewer mistakes)

Encourage the children to explain what they are doing and how they are doing it.

An example activity for the children to evaluate is using a game, such as Angry Birds. This can be played on tablets, but also using the Google Chrome browser on a PC or Mac computer. When they start a level, before they have even fired one bird, they should explain what they are going to do. After they have finished, they can explain if they solved their problem.

- Could they solve it faster? (Removing all the pigs quicker)
- Could they have been more accurate? (Hitting the pigs or blocks exactly as they intended? Did they get the maximum three stars or beat a high score?)
- Could they solve the problem more reliably? (If they repeated the level, would their solution be repeatable?)

Many different games could be used, such as, the Nickelodeon games (www.nick.co.uk/games).

Bite-sized chunks

"Break it down."

We can be overwhelmed by a big problem. The first step is to break it down into smaller, more manageable parts — this is decomposition.

If you ask someone to define 'decomposition', they will probably think about living things, such as leaves, that die and then decompose, returning to the soil in smaller parts. The term decomposition is used in computing too. To break a large problem into smaller parts can enable the children to begin to solve it.

Explain to the children how this can be seen in many areas of the curriculum, for example:

- In a maths lessons a question could be: 'You buy four apples at 20p each, how much change would you have from £1?' The children have to decompose the problem into two parts, firstly working out the total money spent, then working out the change. With computer programs, the main aim of the program needs to be identified. Then, it can be broken into smaller parts and solved.
- In PE, the children may do a gymnastic routine, so we may break the performance into smaller parts of: hand stand, forwards roll, cartwheel, pose, balance, then bow.
- In science lessons, the children may investigate evaporation, so they would find a puddle, make a prediction, draw a circle around it in chalk, measure the diameter and repeat the measurements with time. They could then form conclusions.

There are many problems that we encounter each day. The first step is to break them down into smaller, more manageable parts, then we can begin to solve them.

Teaching tip

Encourage the children to use numbered lists to break problems down, coupled with someone asking them: 'What are you going to do first? What are you going to do next?' If they say the words out loud, they process the information and it will help to clarify their thoughts.

Tablet tip

Recording their voices into a voice-recording app can help the children to process the steps they need to take. Alternatively, they can record a short video 'selfie' to explain what they should do.

Keeping things simple

"What is important and what is not?"

A good description of abstraction is getting rid of the unimportant information. Let's keep things simple.

As a child, I believed in the 'Washing fairy'. I would leave my clothes on the floor and magically, they would reappear, clean and ironed in my drawer. Sadly, I must have grown up, as when I went away to college, the magic ended! Just a joke, but as a child, the details of the clothes being picked up, placed in a washing machine, dried, folded and returned to the drawer, were not important. All I needed to know was: leave clothes on floor, then clothes reappear clean.

Each day, there are many examples where we need to work out 'What is the important information?' and then discard the rest. For example, if someone asks for directions, you may say 'Walk straight ahead and when you reach the next corner, turn right at the supermarket'. You may leave out information, such as, 'Walk straight ahead, past the newsagents, bookmakers, and then the supermarket' or 'Turn right at the supermarket with the red sign, with white letters, made of brick walls and with white windows'.

A great example, which Mark Dorling of CAS has shared, is the London Tube map. All the unimportant information, such as distance between stations, depth of stations, exact location, has been discarded. It simply shows the relationships between the stations and how a passenger can transfer from one line to another.

So, let's have a spring clean and get rid of that unimportant information!

In general . . .

"Now that you know how to do this, can you do that?"

If you use the phrase 'In general . . .' what do you mean? You also might say 'Well, generally, I would . . .' but what do we mean by generalisation?

When I say 'generally', I often think that it's a bit approximate or nondescript: 'Generally, I drive to school'. We can think of generalisation as taking one idea and applying it to a new situation. Explain it to the children with the following examples:

- When closing a car door on the left-hand side, we can generalise to know how to close the door on the right-hand side. When we are shown how to drive one car, we can generalise to drive another. It may not be exactly the same, but we can work it out based on our understanding of driving.
- James Dyson is famous for his vacuum cleaners, where he took the idea of a dust extractor in a sawmill and applied it to vacuum cleaning. He generalised the basic principles and applied them to a new situation.

In computing, once a way of working or a solution to a problem has been found, the programmer may use that learning to apply to a new situation. This not only saves time, but they may have found a really efficient solution, so they can improve their program by applying their prior learning.

Teaching tip

Ask the children to think about doors around the school and other things they operate each day. Can they spot where they are applying previous learning to a new situation? Play 'Charades' – one child has to act out an action and the others guess two places where they may use it.

Tablet tip

Can the children identify the similarities between: Pages and Keynote, Word and PowerPoint or Google Docs and Google Slides? Does Pages have the same icons as Keynote? Could they work out how to use one app, using knowledge from another? Now, could they use an unfamiliar word processing or presentation app and generalise their learning from the other ones?

Progression through pathways

"How do you support teachers to assess their pupils?"

How can we support progression in computing? CAS has created the Progression Pathways for children from Key Stages 1 to 3.

The National Curriculum for computing has certain themes (for example, algorithms, programming, how computers work, communication and e-safety) that progress in very big steps from Key Stage 1 to 2. Mark Dorling and the CAS have broken these steps down in the Progression Pathways Assessment Framework (bit.ly/100computing7a). When identifying an activity, you can 'fit' it across a number of strands in the Pathways, which are colour coded to show progression.

A new version of the Pathways (bit.ly/100computing7b) organises the progression statements into three strands: computer science, information technology and digital literacy, which is an even simpler approach.

So, for example, children may be doing an activity, such as making an app. We can look at the computer science strand and try to 'fit' their learning to a statement. Then, as they continue, it may be possible to see them progress to the next statement. I use the Pathways as a guide to progression and not as an absolute assessment level. It helps non-specialist teachers see some of the smaller steps the children may make.

The Progression Pathways have been amended to include the five areas of computational thinking (see Idea 1). This helps us to see where computational thinking fits within the curriculum (bit.ly/100computing7c).

Algorithms, instructions and recipes

Part 2

Co-ding-a-ling!

"Do you know how to ring a bell? Then let's make music!"

This idea uses a set of hand bells to follow a sequence and play a tune. A set of eight bells can cover an octave and the process of playing a tune can be related to programming.

Hand out a number or colour-coded set of bells to the children. Let them enjoy shaking their bell, learning which number they are ringing and what it sounds like.

- Get students to play simple tunes, such as *Old MacDonald*, which can be played by reading the bell number out in sequence (for example, 4, 4, 4, 1, 2, 2, 1, 6, 6, 5, 5, 4).
- Using PowerPoint, place the codes of the bells to be played on separate slides. (Use a blank slide between each note to distinguish repeated notes.) Play the presentation and ask the children to play their bell as their code appears.
- They may find it hard to name the tune, as it will be quite slow as they try it for the first time. To make it easier, use coded boxes instead of separate slides. In addition, adding the words under the boxes helps them to understand what they are playing.
- Relating the bells activity to computing is really important. When programming, they need to see how the instructions fit together – the notes fit together when they play the bells and hear the tune. Adding the words of the song to the tune is similar to adding 'comments' in the program. Programmers add comments to help themselves and others understand what is happening and what the code is doing. When they can see how the instructions fit together, with the comments adding information, it becomes easier to follow.

Teaching tip

Really encourage the children to see that they are musical as they follow the instructions. The more they practice, the more accurate and precise they will become.

Taking it further

Ask the children to create their own musical instructions, using familiar tunes, for example, 'Three blind mice'. They could use songs from the music charts, to make it more relevant.

Tell me a story

"Are you sitting comfortably? Then I'll begin."

The 'Hero's Journey' is the format of a story used in Greek myths and even *Star Wars*. It follows a particular sequence. Can the children place the story into the correct order?

Teaching tip

Resonate by Nancy Duarte is a fantastic book, where she analyses stories and speeches to identify how they are telling persuasive stories. It uses a clever, visual format to show the different parts. I'd highly recommend reading it and then reviving our own teaching styles. Do we tell good stories in computing?

Tablet tip

Resonate by Nancy Duarte is also an interactive iBook on the iPad. A sample can be downloaded to view the Martin Luther King speech annotated in a very visual way. The Adobe Voice app has several story formats for the user to structure their story. It includes a Hero's Journey format too.

Read a familiar story to the children. This could be a traditional story, such as *The Enormous Turnip,* or a modern story, such as *The Very Hungry Caterpillar*. These have a particular sequence of steps to tell the story. Ask the children to muddle up the order on purpose. Does the story still make sense?

The Hero's Journey follows 16 stages from the beginning to end and many mythical stories followed the pattern. The opening four stages are:

- the call to adventure
- the refusal of the call
- meeting the mentor
- crossing the threshold.

The Star Wars film, *A New Hope,* begins with Luke Skywalker being called to adventure. Can the children find a myth or film that follows the format? Can they retell it in order? Using a simple storyboard, ask them to sketch the scenes.

Relate this learning to algorithms and programs – sometimes the program will not work if the parts are not in the correct order.

Choose your own adventure

"The 'Choose your own adventure' books were a favourite from my youth – you could control your own destiny!"

When I was growing up, the Choose your own adventure books were the height of interactivity. You could decide if you wanted to stay and fight the monster or run away, by turning to particular pages. In computing, this is like 'selection', where decisions are made in programs.

When choosing what to do, we have to make decisions. The Choose your own adventure books were full of decisions. They followed the format of 'If . . . then . . . else.' IF the hero wants to fight the monster, THEN turn to page 67 ELSE turn to page 89. Introduce this concept to the children displayed as a flowchart. Ask:

- Can they think of stories in which the hero needs to make a decision?
- What are the consequences?
- Have they made decisions in their lives?
- What happened after they made a decision?

Use presentation software to make links between parts of a story. The children can write the beginning of the story, then the decision to be made. A 'hyperlink' between the text and another slide can be added. So, when they view the presentation, if they select the link, it will jump to the next part of the story. Do they see how quickly their stories can become complicated? This is relevant to logical thinking and algorithms in computing. The children need to construct the structure for the slides and use logic to link them together correctly.

Fascinating animations of the Choose your own adventure stories showing how the reader can jump to another part of the book can be viewed at bit.ly/100computing10.

Teaching tip

A web-based tool, called Inklewriter (www.inklestudios.com/inklewriter/) enables the children to create these Choose your own adventure stories. They can work individually or it may be more fun for them to work in pairs, taking turns to add the next parts of the stories.

Tablet tip

The Inklewriter tool is web based and can be used on a tablet too. Also, the children can create their stories using the Book creator app. By placing hyperlinks in the text, it can link to other pages in their books.

Telling the future

"This was a fun way to get the children following instructions and thinking about being precise."

Origami fortune tellers are often used by children to reveal a secret answer. They can be used to help the children revise facts too. However, there is a precise sequence of instructions to fold them — following an algorithm.

Teaching tip

Remember, computers need precise instructions in their algorithms (see Idea 2). As humans, we could look at the instructions for the fortune teller and infer what they mean or bring past experience to the situation. Computers need the instructions to be precise, so keep reminding the children to be precise in their explanations and instructions.

Tablet tip

Ask the children to record a short video to show how to make the fortune teller. This can help them remember how to create one. Alternatively, they can use stop-frame animation, for example, 'I can animate' or 'Stop motion pro', to show the steps, taking pictures (an example video http://bit.ly/fortuneteller2).

When folding origami paper fortune tellers, a series of instructions are followed, for example, on the Wikipedia page en.wikipedia.org/wiki/Paper_fortune_teller. However, are these instructions clear? Are there other instructions that could be added to make them more precise?

Ask the children to follow the instructions to make their own fortune tellers. Once complete, they can evaluate how well they have done, for example, are the folds precise? Do the corners meet neatly? Then, can they explain to another child how to make one?

Compare these instructions with others, from the web:

- Origami-fun: bit.ly/100computing11a
- Instructables: bit.ly/100computing11b
- YouTube: bit.ly/fortuneteller1

Ask the children to decorate their fortune tellers with computing pictures on the outside, questions or words on the inside and their definitions on the final panels on the very inside.

Pop chart flowcharts

"This is my favourite lesson."

Songs follow a sequence, often with repeats or loops. Children will enjoy rewriting pop songs as flowcharts. It's time to get in the flow!

Try converting the words of a song into a flowchart. Get the children to choose a song and look at the words. Can they identify questions? For example, in the song *If you're happy and you know it* they could draw boxes and write inside 'Are you happy?' The answer could be 'yes', then they would draw another box and write 'Do you know it?' If the answer was 'yes' again, they could continue their flowchart. If the answer to any of the questions was 'no', then the outcome of the flowchart would be they are not happy or they don't know it.

Songs with repeated choruses or lines make the best flowcharts, for example, *Hey Jude*, MC Hammer's *Can't touch this* or children's songs, like *Heads, Shoulders, Knees and Toes*.

This is a great way of introducing the flowchart symbols used in computing. The different shapes are simple rectangles for each step and then diamonds or rhombuses for decisions, rectangles for processes and rounded rectangles for starting and stopping. Initially, the children can write their flowchart songs by placing the words inside rectangular boxes. Then encourage them to think about the different shapes, for example, 'Is it a question or decision? Then place it in a rhombus.'

Working in pairs helps the process, as the children sing and discuss the steps in the songs.

Tablet tip

Ask the children to draw their flowcharts using pen and paper and then, using the camera on the tablet, capture images. These can be displayed for the class to see. It can be quicker for them to sketch the flowchart on paper than to use software. However, by using the flowchart shapes in presentation apps (such as Keynote or Google Slides) they can add animations to display each step, while playing in time to the music.

Taking it further

Using the TV show *The X Factor* as a model, ask four children to act as judges to evaluate how well the children have converted the song to a flowchart. Can they offer advice and improvements to make them more efficient flowcharts?

Sticky note flowcharts

"Sticky notes are great for writing short notes, great for planning flowcharts too!"

To help the planning of a flowchart, sticky notes are really useful for adding the separate steps. The different colours really help the children think about the process.

Sticky notes help us to remember things; we can use them to give a note to someone and to pass on small pieces of information. We can also use them in our flowchart planning. Each step can be placed on to a separate sticky note and the children can then rearrange them into an order. Try using them in the following ways:

- The first note could be 'Start'. If the flowchart was to show making a sandwich, the children may suggest the next step as 'Butter bread', but then another child might argue that you need to get bread first, so the first step could be 'Get bread'. The sticky notes allow steps to be moved around and for a discussion of what should come next.
- Decisions can also be introduced, such as, 'Have you got bread?' if YES then do this or if NO then do that. This can be written on the sticky note and the next steps placed under and to the side of the note.
- You can introduce different colour notes, for example, green for 'Start' or pink for a decision. Also, cutting shapes out of the sticky notes can help the children to identify, for example, a rhombus for a decision or rounded rectangle for 'Start' and 'Stop'.

This will have you in stitches

"Time for some social knitworking!"

Knitting and programming have many similarities. If you say knitting to anyone, they may say 'knit one, purl one', which are examples of instructions we follow in the knitting algorithm.

My Uncle Norman is a famous knitter and weaver. I'd been thinking about programming when he visited and started to show the different patterns in his jumpers. Each pattern had a name, a purpose and a set of instructions to create it. Also, he took different patterns from people and put them together to solve a problem. This struck me as the work of the skilled programmer, who knows the problem they want to solve, so they use parts of code and put them together. The patterns showed lines of instructions, using a specific vocabulary: knit, purl, increase, cast off.

When I tried to learn to knit, I found it very difficult. Books did not help, but videos did. Asking people to show me had a wide range of outcomes: asking someone new to knitting really helped, but asking a knitting expert proved frustrating. They could not remember what it was like to be a beginner and became frustrated, so I became frustrated. It dawned on me that sometimes, showing people new to computing or tablets can be frustrating for both of you, if you cannot empathise and remember what it was like when starting to learn.

To get children interested, try finger knitting so they can make something without the need for knitting needles. A length of thick wool is needed for each child (wind the wool around your hand approximately 25 times). Then show the finger knitting video from the British Craft Council (bit.ly/fingerknit). It may help to pause the video if they need to catch up.

Teaching tip

The first time you try finger knitting with the class you will see a range of abilities. Some children will pick it up straight away, some need a little help to correct an error (debugging) and others will get frustrated and give up. So it is with programming, where some find it easier than others. The key to success with both knitting and programming is perseverance.

Tablet tip

Ask the children to work in pairs to capture a video of how they finger knit. They could follow the style of the video from the British Craft Council or try their own. Tools such as iMovie allow 'picture-in-picture' videos to be created, so the children can narrate over their own video, adding information and evaluation.

You put your left arm in

"That's what it's all about!"

Action songs like the *Hokey Cokey* have easily recognised moves, which go in time with the music. These are fun examples of algorithms that can get the children up and moving.

If you say the words 'You put your left arm in, you put your left arm out' most people will pick up straightaway that you're doing the *Hokey Cokey*. There are many songs which have repeated lines, and actions, for example, *Dingle-dangle scarecrow*, *The wheels on the bus* or pop songs, such as the *Macarena*.

By getting the children to do the actions to songs, while singing the words, they can break it down into steps. Using mini whiteboards, get them to write the instructions to do the dance.

With the *Hokey Cokey*, the instructions could be:

1. You put your left arm in
2. You put your left arm out
3. In
4. Out
5. In
6. Out
7. You shake it all about

Some children may recognise the repeat and refine their instructions to be:

1. Repeat 3 (left arm in then left arm out)
2. Shake it all about

Let the children choose a pop song (one with or without actions). Can they create a dance routine to match the music?

Bonus idea ★

Different countries have folk dances, for example, a Scottish ceilidh has dances with specific instructions for the dancers to follow. Challenge the children to investigate the dances for another country, create a set of instructions and then teach the class.

The story spine

"Once upon a time . . ."

Acting out a story can be difficult as it is such an open-ended task. We can guide the children by adding a structure or spine to the story. This can be an example of an algorithm, following steps.

Pixar, the creators of the Toy Story films, have '22 Rules of Storytelling' (bit.ly/100computing16a). Rules can help to structure problem solving. Can the children identify where these rules have been used in the Pixar films?

Improvisation, coming up with stories on the spot, can thrill the children and they can act out different scenes. However, it can also be very difficult, so using a structure can help. This is related to computing through following a sequence of steps in a particular order.

Using a structure called the 'Story spine', the children can invent a story and improvise a particular sequence.

The 'Story spine' (bit.ly/100computing16b) by Kenn Adams looks like this:

- Once upon a time . . .
- Every day . . .
- but, one day . . .
- because of that . . .
- because of that . . .
- because of that . . .
- Until, finally . . .
- and ever since then . . .

The children love trying to make a more outrageous story than their friends' stories.

Ensure the link to computing is made by talking about 'sequences' or 'steps', and the need to place them in a precise order to create a story.

Teaching tip

Make it very clear to the children that sequencing the story is like an algorithm. You need to follow steps, to tell the story in the correct order. By changing the order of the steps, you would change the algorithm. Can they think of a well-known story, rearrange the order of the main scenes and then consider if it still works as a good story? For example, in Cinderella, if she married the prince, before he had met her at the ball, it would change the story and it would not make sense.

Tablet tip

Using an app, such as Shadow puppet, the children can add still images and narration. So, they can either act out the scenes from the story or gather them from the web. Once placed in order in the app, the children can still work in pairs to add the narration.

Story dice – introducing variables

"Every roll of the dice can change your story"

Rory's Story Cubes have been a favourite tool for creativity and for bridging the analogue and digital ways of telling stories. They can introduce variables into a story.

Teaching tip

There are different sets of Rory's Story Cubes, such as 'Actions' and 'Voyages'. Asking the children to think of their own symbols for dice can really engage them. Ask them to create cardboard nets, to which they can add their symbols before telling new stories.

Tablet tip

There is a Rory's Story Cubes app, which can enable the children to play with dice on the tablet. This is useful for displaying on the projector screen, for whole-class activities. Alternatively, using the camera on the tablet, a photo of the dice could be captured. Using the live feed from the camera, while connected to the projector, can enable the class to see the dice being rolled and see the live outcomes.

When I first saw Rory's Story Cubes (www.storycubes.com), I thought they would be great for my children. There are nine dice in each set, and each dice has a different symbol/picture on each face. The children can roll the dice and use the symbols to create a story. Try the following ideas:

- Begin with just three dice and ask the children to create simple stories, for example, 'Once upon a time, there was an alien, who saw a sheep and went over a bridge'. By questioning the children, the story can expand: 'What was the alien's name? Where did they come from? Where does the bridge go?' This helps them develop their questioning skills.
- To link to computing, say that each of the dice is a variable in the story. Rolling one of the dice again produces a new part of the story. Highlight the word 'variable'.
- Challenge the children to think of a well-known story and choose a character. Can they replace that character with another character from a different story? Could they swap an object in the story, for example, 'Jack and the beanstalk' could become 'Jack and the light bulb'?
- Explain that dice are used in many games, like 'Dungeons and Dragons', they can alter the outcome of a game and change the story – all controlled by variables.

Shopping list

"Don't forget the milk!"

When introducing variables, we need to find practical ways to demonstrate how they can be used. A shopping list game is a fun way of keeping a score and varying the numbers of items on the list.

Organise the children into teams and sit them in columns, one behind another. Each child is given either a person or object as their name, taken from a particular story. Then, as the story is read, every time their name is mentioned, they have to run around their team and back to their place. Stories like *The Enormous Turnip*, or *The Gruffalo* by Julia Donaldson, work well because they include characters which are repeatedly mentioned.

Alternatively, make up your own story based on a shopping list. For example, you could say, 'Once upon a time, the school's cook went to the supermarket. They bought a tomato'. At this point the children in each team who are labelled as 'tomatoes' need to run around their team and back to their seat. The first one back to their seat gets a point. Carry on: 'The cook also bought an onion' etc.

The scores are examples of variables. Each time a team gets a point, the score can increase by one. This could be represented by numbers, by adding bean bags to a bucket or by placing a marble in a jar. Other variables can be introduced in the shopping list, for example, they buy two tomatoes, so the child called 'tomatoes' needs to run around twice. The same can be continued for four potatoes and so on. Ask the children to add their own ideas, such as, if the word 'supermarket' is mentioned then everyone can run!

Teaching tip

When inventing the story, try to highlight the word 'variables' (not vegetables!) to show that, in this example, it is the number of items or score that changes.

Tablet tip

'Remember the milk' is an online 'To do' list, also available as an app. It helps people to have a reminder list, which can be accessed from anywhere with an Internet connection. Would particular children benefit from a tool like this? Can the children think of any disadvantages to using the app? Does the list follow a sequence, for example, can they order the to do list into a logical order?

What's the time, Mr. Wolf?

"What's the time, Mr. Wolf? . . . Dinner time!"

The game of 'What's the time, Mr. Wolf?' involves a loop of asking the question until the wolf says 'Dinner time!' So, can the children program the game to involve the loop and a random variable? Planning on paper first, followed by adding the commands on the computer, will let them try.

There are many games that involve repeating actions until a final step. With 'What's the time, Mr. Wolf?' one child (Mr. Wolf) stands facing a wall, while the other children move forwards, asking 'What's the time, Mr. Wolf?'. This step is repeated, as a loop of instructions, until the children either reach Mr. Wolf or Mr. Wolf says 'Dinner time!' and runs after the other children. Try using the game in the following ways:

- Play the game with the children and let them see the way it repeats, with the stages looping around, until it is 'Dinner time'.
- Ask the children to write the instructions using a simple numbered list. They should be able to see where the steps are repeated – identifying the loops.
- As a next step ask them to draw the flowchart, showing the loop more clearly as the lines go around, asking 'Is it dinner time?', if 'Yes' chase after the children, if 'No' keep moving towards Mr. Wolf, asking 'What's the time?'
- Can the children think of other games with loops?

Human fruit machine

"This is great fun, the children like to pretend they are a fruit machine and the others enjoy guessing the outcomes."

A 'human fruit machine' is where three people sit in a row, each with a bowl of fruit in front of them. On the count of three, they all pick up a piece of fruit at random and scores are applied for different combinations!

Before you begin, ask the class to decide upon the scoring system. Divide the class into two teams and give each child a go at starting the machine. Ask the children to draw a record of the draws, for example, oranges in columns 1 and 2 and an apple in column 3. Once 20 draws have taken place, ask them if they think it is a truly random process. Does one of the three people choosing the fruit favour a particular type of fruit? If so, after the next 20 draws, has that person changed bias towards another piece of fruit?

The conversations about being random are really interesting. One story I share with the children is about a friend of mine. When the National Lottery was first introduced he bought a ticket with numbers one, two, three, four, five and six. We all laughed at him, but he said, 'Well, if it is a truly random selection of numbers, then why cannot one to six appear?' That did silence us. So, ask the children to think about whether it could ever happen that numbers one to six could be drawn. An organisation to help teach children about computing is 'Code Club'. They have developed resources, which schools can use, which include a fruit machine example. (Visit www.codeclub.org.uk and select 'Projects'. After a quick, free registration, you can access the resources.) It is definitely worth considering setting up a Code Club and thinking about inviting volunteers of parents and local businesses into school to help with the teaching of coding.

Tablet tip

Scratch was developed by the Massachusetts Institute of Technology (MIT) to teach programming. A version for the iPad has been produced for younger users, called ScratchJr. However, there is a version of Scratch which can be used on the iPad, called 'Pyonkee'. This can be used to create a fruit machine, using the Code Club resources.

Bonus idea ★

Hold a classroom tournament of 'Rock, Paper, Scissors' then ask them to toss a coin and choose heads or tails. When the games are complete, ask the children which game they considered to be more random. They will most likely choose the coin game, as there is more human choice in 'Rock, Paper, Scissors'. Ask them why they think we cannot be completely random? Can a computer be completely random?

Is this your card?

"Is this your card? No? Is this your card? No? Is this your card? No?"

Card tricks are a great way of introducing variables, and also iteration, which can be described as repeating a process to get towards a desired goal.

Take a set of playing cards and choose 18 cards. Ask somebody to choose one and then show them every card until they say 'That's my card'. They won't feel there has been anything magical, just a simple process. It is also not a very efficient process. If you were to place 18 cards into three columns of six and ask, 'Is your card in this column?' you could eliminate twelve cards in the first go. Then by placing the remaining six cards into two columns and asking again, 'Is your card in this column?' you would be down to the last three.

This act of repeating a process to get towards the desired goal (in this case, finding the card) is called iteration. There are many games that involve iteration, for example, a football tournament involves playing football matches until a winning team is found. The children will be familiar with the idea, but may not have realised that they are repeating a process to get to the final outcome.

Give the children time to struggle with the card trick to find a quicker way of laying out the cards and asking questions to iterate down to the last card. It may be that they lay the cards out in columns of three to begin with and then ask questions.

Explain to the children that computers can be used to crack codes, such as the great work carried out during World War Two at Bletchley Park by Alan Turing. The computer may iterate to find a solution to a difficult code.

Time to get dressed

"You're never fully dressed without a smile."

Getting dressed is an idea children understand. From a young age, they've been dressed by others and encouraged to learn to do it for themselves. Actually, there is a long list of instructions that need to be sequenced. You cannot put your shoes on before your socks.

Play the party game 'Getting dressed'. There are a number of items that the player needs to put on, before they are allowed to eat a bar of chocolate – using a knife and fork! For example, they need to put on a coat, scarf, hat and then gloves, before beginning to try to eat the chocolate. Meanwhile, the rest of the children are taking turns to roll a dice. If they score a six, then they are the new player. They have to get the coat, scarf, hat and gloves from the previous player and put them on in that order. Once dressed, they can start eating, until the next six is rolled. Emphasise that they must follow the sequence. If it is proving too difficult, try reducing the number of items or breaking the chocolate into small pieces.

Use sequence cards to reinforce the learning from the game. Ask the children to look at the cards (one picture of a piece of clothing on each card). Ask them to sequence the cards into order, for example, trousers, socks then shoes. Now can they begin to create a series of questions: 'Have you got your left sock on?' If 'No' then 'Put your left sock on.' If 'Yes', then 'Have you got your right sock on?'

There are several 'dress the teddy' type activities online (for example, bit. ly/100computing22). This could lead to using the Scratch software to make a program for getting dressed.

Teaching tip

The children may have a discussion about the order of clothes they put on. Some may put their socks on before trousers or they may put left sock on before right. This can make the activity really fun, as they discuss what they presume is the same for everyone. Hopefully, though, they do realise that shoes need to follow socks!

Tablet tip

Ask the children to create their own sequence cards for the 'Getting dressed' game. By putting on the clothes in order: coat, scarf, hat and gloves, they could take a photo at each stage. They can then place the images into a presentation tool, such as PowerPoint or Keynote, and sequence the pictures or experiment with mixing up the order.

Getting dressed with subroutines

"Tying your shoelaces, buttoning a shirt, brushing your hair, cleaning your teeth – these have instructions, but can we make them more efficient?"

When tying your shoelaces, you repeat a series of instructions for your left shoe and then for your right shoe. Instead of writing the instructions again, we can introduce a 'mini' set of instructions for the tying, which can be repeated for each shoe. This is called a subroutine.

When you tie a shoelace, you are carrying out a series of instructions, which has taken much practice to perfect. Someone taught you by showing you, using language that you could understand and repeating the instructions over again for each shoe. The instructions for each shoe are the same, even though one is your left and one your right shoe.

Ask the children if they can think of any times where they need to repeat a series of instructions. For example, if they need to sharpen three pencils, what would their instructions be?

1. Place pencil in pencil sharpener.
2. Turn ten times.
3. Take pencil out and check if it is sharp.

Then they might try the next pencil. So, if they were writing the instructions, they could write:

1. Place pencil in pencil sharpener.
2. Turn ten times.
3. Take pencil out and check if it is sharp.
4. Next pencil.
5. Place pencil in pencil sharpener.
6. Turn ten times.
7. Take pencil out and check if it is sharp.
8. Next pencil.

9. Place pencil in pencil sharpener.
10. Turn ten times.
11. Take pencil out and check if it is sharp.

It can be seen that a repeat could be used to repeat the instructions, for example:

1. Repeat three times.
2. Place pencil in pencil sharpener.
3. Turn ten times.
4. Take pencil out and check if it is sharp.
5. Next pencil.

What happens though if later in the day (or program) more pencils need sharpening?

Another way of writing this would be to define a subroutine named: Pencil sharpening

1. Define 'pencil sharpening' as Place pencil in pencil sharpener, turn ten times, take pencil out and check if it is sharp.
2. Repeat three times 'Pencil sharpening'. Other activities could happen next before then need to do 'Pencil sharpening' again (without the need to write the instructions again).

Initially this may seem longer for the children, so explain that this method of writing 'subroutines' can make longer programs more efficient.

Think about buttoning up a shirt. The instructions for one button could be repeated for five buttons or a subroutine for buttoning could be created.

If the children write instructions for drawing a capital letter using the LOGO language or using the Scratch software, they will see that it takes a number of instructions. If they were then going to write the same letter three times, then maybe they would think a 'repeat' command would be better. However, if they had to spell out a name where the instructions for different letters are used, such as 'ANNA', then it could be more efficient to have the letters A and N defined as subroutines, which could be called when needed.

Travelling to school

"Follow the yellow brick road, follow the yellow brick road, follow, follow, follow, follow . . ."

In the story *The Wizard of Oz* the characters are told to follow the yellow brick road. This could be an instruction for a robot to continue on the road until they reach the destination. However, the children's journeys to school may be more complicated, so they need to think of a program to get there.

Get each child to use a Google map to write the instructions for their route to school. Demonstrate how the distance between two places can be found. Right-clicking on a location brings up the menu for 'Directions to here' and 'Directions from here'. The two locations on the route to school can be selected and it will offer a route and the distance.

The BeeBot is a programmable robot, which is popular in schools. The instructions can be entered via the BeeBot's keypad and then off it goes. Then the process of debugging can occur, to ensure it follows the correct path.

- Ask the children to create simple routes for the BeeBot around the school by placing pieces of A4 paper on the floor (stuck together with tape). These are a fun and cheap way of creating puzzles to solve.
- A great idea (from Paul Hutton) is to project the Google satellite map of the school's local area on to a wall, then use large pieces of paper to trace the outlines of the roads, school and important buildings. This large paper map can be placed on the floor and the BeeBot can be programmed to follow the roads.
- The children could create a fantasy map to show the way to Oz. If the class is reading a particular story, this could form the theme, for example, the route the BFG travels from the giants' land to London and then around the city.

Sort it out

"Oh no! I've dropped my cards. How can we sort them out?"

Begin the lesson with a comedy, slapstick dropping of a set of playing cards. Once the children have stopped laughing, ask them 'How can we sort them back into order?' By dividing the cards into small sets and sharing them with the children, let them discover their best method of sorting the cards.

Tommy Cooper made his name by performing magic tricks badly. Everyone knew that something was going to go wrong as he walked onto the stage. By beginning the lesson with a deliberate mistake you can ask the children to help you.

As the playing cards flutter to the floor – oh no! Ask 'Can you help me sort them out?' The children can collect the cards in groups, so that each group has the same number. What will be their strategy? They could place all the numbered cards together in a line, then the picture cards. They might sort them into the different suits first, and then place them in order.

In their groups, they should choose one person to be the 'Instructor'. Then each of the group should take a card and stand in a random order. The instructor then gives instructions to the group for two children to swap places. They swap and then the next instruction is given. Can they sort the cards into the correct order, by swapping two cards at a time? What is their criteria for selecting the two cards? Swap a larger number with smaller, until the smallest number is on the left-hand side?

There are many examples to teach computing without using a computer in the booklet 'CSUnplugged' (csunplugged.org). It can be downloaded for free and will help the children with their understanding of different concepts.

Teaching tip

It may help to display the order for a set of cards, for those who do not know or to help the children as they sort them. Make the task simpler by using fewer cards or by giving cards from the same suit to each group. By mixing up the suits, they need to put the cards into order and also create a priority order for the suits, for example, they may have ordered the cards for hearts, but which suit are they going to place next? In the game of 'Bridge' the order can be spades, hearts, diamonds, then clubs.

Tablet tip

There are many sorting apps for younger children, such as Sorting 1 by TinyHands. They can practise placing objects or animals into a sequence. Older children can play games like Sorting Books by Qnuouo, which has a more age-appropriate context.

Building in the dark

"Put the red one on the black one. Which red one? Which black one? What do you mean?"

Many years ago, as part of a leadership course, we tried to communicate by describing different pictures to a partner. The problem was we were sitting back-to-back and so a shared vocabulary, clear instructions and clarifying questions were crucial. This is a great activity to do using a few LEGO bricks.

Teaching tip

If LEGO bricks are not available, then use simple drawings. The first child can sketch two triangles and then the second can draw them. Another idea is they could describe a well-known object, such as a fork, but they are not allowed to mention its name or purpose. The precise instructions should tell their partner what to draw.

Tablet tip

The LEGO movie has a great sequence on instructions, where the hero follows 'Instructions for life and getting everybody to like you'. Ask the children to recreate instructions using stop-frame animation apps, for example, I can animate or Zu3D. They could even use LEGO minifigures to be the stars of their movie.

Making LEGO models really gets the children excited. If someone else was giving the instructions, would it be as easy?

LEGO bricks come in different colours and sizes. Imagine a white brick, with four studs on top in a line (4 x 1). What would you call it? The colour is the easy part! When you have agreed on colour and brick name (four-studder or four by one) how are the two bricks going to be joined? On top of each other could mean there are no overlapping parts. If there are overlapping parts, how many? A common language of instruction needs to be developed.

Place the children back-to-back and give each child four LEGO bricks (they each must have the same type). The first child puts their bricks together and then describes this to their partner. Neither child must turn around to look. They must use a common language to describe what to do and to clarify the instructions. After one minute, let them compare models and see if they are the same. Now try it again three times, before swapping roles. Do they get more accurate and quicker as they develop their common vocabulary?

Make sure the children understand that computers need precise instructions. They are developing their precision, using a commonly understood language.

Flip-flap-folding

"Folding clothes is not a favourite activity for anyone – however, it involves a sequence of instructions and evaluation to see how well they have done."

Very rarely will the children have thought about how they fold clothes. Also, once they have tried it, they can evaluate how neatly they have done it. Add an element of competition and they enjoy seeing who can fold fastest and neatest!

'The Big Bang Theory' is an American comedy programme, which involves a character called Sheldon who is very particular about how he does his laundry. In one episode, he folds the washing using a plastic tool. It proved so popular that people on social media wanted to know where to purchase one. I tried the activity out with teachers and was asked the same question. An example can be seen online (bit.ly/100computing27). When folding clothes, a simple set of instructions means that the folding activity can be carried out quickly, but also with more consistency.

- Choose four children to fold a set of t-shirts. Start a stopwatch for one minute and see how many shirts can be folded within that time. Once complete and shirts counted, ask the children to evaluate how well they have been folded. They would need to decide upon the criteria – symmetrical, neat, piled together in a compact shape? Next ask another four children to fold the clothes. Can they fold quicker and more accurately?
- Ask the children to create the instructions for folding by drawing images for each step. This is a difficult skill, as the pictures need to clearly convey the actions. How would the instructions differ for a jumper, a pair of trousers or a pair of socks?

Teaching tip

When the children are creating the instructions for folding an item of clothing, give them each a piece of A4 paper folded to give eight panels in which to draw. Fold the paper in half, in half and in half again, before opening it out. There should be eight rectangles, divided by the folds.

Tablet tip

Ask the children to draw the instructions using the Doink animation app. This can create a series of drawings, which will be animated, similar to a 'flick' book. Alternatively, a series of photographs could be added to a video app, like iMovie. Then the images can have a narrated track added, to explain how to fold clothes.

The computer says 'Yes' – programming ideas

Part 3

Scratching an itch

"Today we are going to Scratch."

The Scratch software is used for programming by many schools. Its colourful blocks of code invite the children to make their own programs. Where can you find further resources to learn about it? Which apps are similar for learning on tablets?

Scratch is probably the most popular software for teaching programming in primary schools. It has been developed by the Lifelong Kindergarten Group at MIT and it is free (scratch.mit.edu). Animations, interactive stories and games can be created by placing the colourful blocks of code together. Unlike programming using a text language, the blocks enable the children to add commands without errors of misspelling or commas in the wrong places.

As many schools use Scratch, there is a growing community around it, and many great resources:

- Scratch Ed (scratched.gse.harvard.edu) dedicated to teaching with Scratch, they have created a curriculum to support the learning (scratched.gse.harvard.edu/guide).
- Barefoot Computing (barefootcas.org.uk) resources from Computing at School.
- Code Club is an organisation to encourage schools to set up clubs for children to learn about programming (codeclub.org.uk/).

Currently, Scratch has two versions. Version 1.4 can be downloaded and installed on to the computer. Version 2.0 has been designed to work online. There is also an 'Offline editor' for Version 2.0, allowing it to run when not connected to the Internet. Version 2.0 has some extra blocks, for example, to enable the camera on the computer to be used. A version of Scratch is available for the iPad, called the 'Pyonkee' app (softumeya.com/pyonkee/en).

The magic box

"Think of all the things you put into your brain? What comes out?"

If you told children that the answer was 18 and the starting number was 3, how could they get to the answer? What is happening in the 'function machine' sitting between the two numbers?

Create a huge 'magic box' function machine!

- Get a large box covered in a sheet of foil (big enough for a child to fit behind).
- Choose a child before the lesson and explain how the box will work.
- Begin with fun things, such as passing a teaspoon to the left of the box and the child passing a tablespoon out of the right.
- Pretend to turn up the volume and pass a teaspoon in; they could pass a ladle out.
- Ask the children to explain what is happening inside the box.
- Now pass numbers of items into the magic box, for example, two in and four out.
- Try to highlight the words 'input' and 'output'.
- Let the children play their own magic box game, with different items or numbers.

Using simple spreadsheets, ask the children to create function machines. They should put the input number in the first column, colour the next cell along to make it look like a box, and put the target number in the third column. Then they need to work out an equation to get from, say, 3 to 18. For example, = A1 * 6 (the number in cell A1 is multiplied by 6).

The idea of inputs and outputs can be linked to computers. The keyboard and mouse are input devices, putting information into the computer. The screen, printer or speakers are output devices, giving information out. On tablet computers the screen responds to touch, so it is an input and output device.

Teaching tip

With the spreadsheet idea, it may be easier for the children to add numbers in column A and then an equation in column B. They would swap computers with a partner and they would try to guess what was happening to the numbers.

Tablet tip

There are function machine-style apps available (Function machine by Natural Maths), which let the children try out different numbers to deduce what the machine is doing to the numbers.

Strictly come dancing

"Keeeeeeeep dancing!"

Television dance programmes have become very popular. The dances follow sets of instructions, which are executed in time to the music. Now it's time to put on your dancing shoes!

Teaching tip

There are several dance video games for consoles, such as the 'Just Dance' series (just-dance.ubi.com). The children could look at the sequences of different dance moves. Then they could take pictures of themselves dancing and import them into the Scratch software, to be programmed.

Tablet tip

Ask the children to create a dance book. Using the Book Creator app, they could research different styles of dance and place an image and short description on each page. On a facing page, they could insert a video of themselves performing the dance or an impression of it. Alternatively, include football or gymnastic moves. A football trick has specific movements for the body and feet, similar to a dance. A video of the child performing a movement with a description could be added to their books.

In the TV programme, *Strictly come dancing*, the dancers perform different types of dances, such as the waltz, which follows a three-step pattern. They must follow the instructions carefully and precisely, in order to gain a high score.

Show the children some of the basic dance steps for different dances (www.dancing4beginners. com/dance-steps-for-waltz.htm). You may struggle to get the boys and girls to dance together, so they could practise a simple move in rows, facing the front of the room.

Let the children invent their own dance moves. They could create four steps, which can be repeated. Once they have decided upon on the moves, how can they write them down? Could they sketch the outline of the feet and draw arrows to show the movements.

Can the children be dance teachers? In pairs, using their dance steps, ask one child to instruct the other. They should focus on being accurate and clear in the way they describe the steps.

For inspiration, they could watch videos of ballroom dancers, break dancers or 'B-Boy' dancers, looking at the combinations of moves and how they join them together. This could be thought of as subroutines of dance moves, which are called and combined to make the whole dance.

I'm board

"Board games are a great way of introducing rules. Some games are easier to understand than others; are the rules simpler or more precise? It's time to play!"

At the end of term, we used to have a games day. The children would bring board games in from home. We really enjoyed the interaction and the buzz around the room. There's decomposition, abstraction, generalisation, algorithmic thinking and evaluation. So, why wait until the end of term?

Ask the children to bring in board games. They may have played one recently or they may need to search around the house. If they cannot find one, then they can share, as most board games are aimed at small groups. That's what I like about them. They encourage communication and collaboration.

Let the children enjoy playing the games, then ask them to write ten rules for the game. They could write each rule on a separate strip of paper. Now, can they rank them into a top ten order, with the most important rule first? This always encourages debate.

Video games will often have an 'in-game tutorial', to show the player the rules and how to play. These can be crucial to the player succeeding and persevering with the game. As the player begins, there is not a lot of text explaining what to do, front-loading with information. They may start to play and it could pause to explain what to do next. This can be similar to the children explaining how to play a board game. If they were to sit down and talk through all the rules of a game such as Monopoly, they would never get started. By introducing the rules as they play, they become relevant and can keep the game flowing. It is important that they are precise and clear in their explanations.

Teaching tip

Letting the children 'break the rules' of the games can be an interesting insight into gameplay. When they change the rules, does it make the games better? Do they just get frustrated, because they do not understand how to play anymore? Could it be that the classic games have lasted because the rules have been developed and refined to improve gameplay?

Tablet tip

Using a spreadsheet app, such as Numbers, Excel or Google Sheets, children can play Battleships. Instead of communicating face-to-face, players, could try messaging using email or Skype. This would mean they could be playing while in the classroom or even from another place in the world!

Debugging

"All the games are broken! Can you help fix them"?

Video games and computers sometimes go wrong. The device might crash or not behave as it is supposed to. We may use the term 'bug', but can we fix it?

Debugging is a phrase used in computing to mean fix or improve solutions to problems.

The children can play a debugging game:

- In pairs, one child is the robot moving around the room and the other child is the one giving commands (the controller).
- The robot can follow the commands by moving forward (1 pace), back (1 pace), left turn (by 90°) and right turn (by 90°).
- The controller writes a series of commands, for example, forwards, right, forwards, left, back. If the program worked correctly, the robot would follow the commands exactly as they were given.
- However, the robot chooses one of the commands to do incorrectly, for example, move forwards instead of backwards.
- The controller gives the commands to the robot and the robot moves using the 'bugged' commands.
- Can the controller guess which commands are not being carried out correctly? Can they 'fix the bugs'?
- Make the game more complicated by using different numbers of paces, or different size turns.

Ask the children to create a game (using Scratch or Mozilla Appmaker) where a character is moved around a maze. The control keys could be mixed up. Once programmed, the children could swap and see if they can debug the games.

What's the context?

"Context is essential to learning. We will often theme lessons around contexts like space, pirates or a book, such as *War Horse*, and computing lessons should have a strong context too."

Using a strong context in your lessons really makes a difference. The TPACK model below shows how content, technical and pedagogical knowledge are all needed, but within a context. Using this model, you can evaluate your approaches to learning.

Ask the children to name a video game and tell you its theme. For example, the Skylanders games use different storylines to take the player through a series of levels. The games introduce knowledge about the characters and their world, technical content of how to play the levels and then an approach to how the game can teach the player the skills they need. The combination of the three areas of knowledge is very important for success.

When teaching a computing topic, such as algorithms, we need to ensure the children develop the content knowledge – what is an algorithm? Where are they found? We need to have the technical knowledge, for example, how to recognise an algorithm, how to follow the steps. The third part is our pedagogical approach, that is, how are we going to teach about algorithms? This might, for example, be through sorting games, instructions, flowcharts. Again, it's the combination of all three areas that will enable learning to happen.

TPACK (www.tpack.org/)represents: Content knowledge (CK), Technical knowledge (TK) And Pedagogical knowledge (PK). Where the three areas overlap is called TPACK. The vital addition surrounding the diagram is a large circle with the word 'CONTEXTS'.

Teaching tip

Think about a lesson you taught recently. Can you identify the content knowledge, technical knowledge and pedagogical knowledge you encountered? What was the context which made it relevant to the children?

Taking it further

Visit the TPACK website (www.tpack.org/) and register for a free account. There are many explanations of the TPACK model and research discussions too. How would you explain the model to another teacher at your school? How would you explain it to parents or children?

IFTTT

"If this happens then what will happen next?"

In programming, we think about events or something happening as a consequence of an action. For example, 'if the score reaches zero, then say game over'. These events are used for many purposes, so we need to get the children thinking 'If this happens, then that happens'.

IFTTT stands for 'If this, then that'. It is an online a tool used to make something happen based on another event occurring. For example, you can set up your mobile phone to send yourself a message when you arrive at a certain location. Even the heating in your house can be switched on, as you are approaching home! IF I am one mile from home, THEN switch on the heating. Develop this way of thinking with your children:

- Play the 'Consequences' game with the children in groups of four. The first child simply draws a head on a piece of paper, then folds the paper over their drawing and passes it on to the next child, who draws a body. The next person draws the legs, and the last child draws the feet. When they open the paper out, it should look like a very strange person or creature.
- Develop the game to tell a story. The first sentence could read 'Once there was a . . .' The children write a word, then fold the paper over and pass it on. Then continue the story, 'Who wanted to see a . . .' etc.
- Reinforce the idea of consequences with the children's programming. IF the player presses the space bar THEN make the character jump.
- The 'ELSE' option can be added too: IF the player presses the space bar THEN make the character jump ELSE keep moving to the right. This is used in programming: in the Scratch software there is an 'IF' block and also an 'IF' block with an 'ELSE' in it.

The 'Hour of Code'

"The 'Hour of Code' is a great way to enthuse children about programming!"

Why is coding important? We can tell the children why, but wouldn't it be great to hear it from a celebrity? What about hearing from someone who has created something amazing?

The 'Hour of Code' aims to get children excited about coding. The website uk.code.org has a great introductory video, where famous people explain how they first became interested and why they think it is important.

The 'Hour of Code' has been created to encourage people to hold an event, to introduce computer science and 'demystify code' (hourofcode.com/uk).

There are more and more resources being produced to support the Hour of Code, for example:

- The UK Hour of Code website has resources using Disney's Frozen characters: (studio. code.org/s/frozen/stage/1/puzzle/1).
- Tynker has several examples, based on the Scratch blocks style: (www.tynker.com/hour-of-code/).
- Microsoft has resources based on their Kodu game-making software: (www.kodugamelab. com/hour-of-code/).

Each year a special week is selected especially for running Hour of Code events, so why don't you plan it into your school calendar? Can you encourage parents or local businesses to become involved? Could you start a weekly club to develop the coding skills of the children, after they have tried their 'Hour of Code'?

Teaching tip

Children can really benefit from teaching others how to code. Get your children to lead lessons for other classes. They could be digital leaders in your school, organising events or running a lunchtime club. Think how you can use their enthusiasm and skills in coding.

Tablet tip

A great learning tool is called Lightbot, where a robot is directed around mazes in order to reach a goal (lightbot.com/hocflash.html). It can be played on PC and Mac and also on tablets. The Lightbot Hour of Code apps (lightbot.com/) can be found for all types of tablet computer.

Changing the news

". . . and finally, here's an amusing news story."

Creating news stories is good fun and can support literacy. However, by subtly adjusting news webpages, can the children work out the truthful stories from the fake ones?

Mozilla, the organisation most widely known for creating the Firefox web browser, is keen to educate everyone about the web. Its mission is to enable people to 'create the web we want' and not leave it to big powerful organisations to be in charge of the content we see. Mozilla harnesses the power of a large community of people who want to teach webmaking skills and digital literacy. To 'teach the web', Mozilla has created tools which form part of the 'Webmaker' resources (webmaker.org/en-US/explore). One of these tools is called X-ray Goggles (goggles.webmaker.org) and another is called Thimble (see Idea 37).

X-ray Goggles works by allowing any webpage to be edited and changed, for example, using the BBC News webpages, you can change the headlines! To get started, you need an up-to-date web browser. Make sure the bookmark bar is displayed, then follow the instructions on the webpage to load the X-ray Goggles button.

Take time to play with different webpages and see how the HTML code is written. Play around by changing the text, then searching for images to replace ones in the webpage.

Choose a news story and take a screenshot of the webpage. Then, using X-ray Goggles, change the headline or the image and take a screenshot of the modified one. In the lesson, show the children both stories; can they work out which one is real? What are the clues that help them decide?

Tablet tip

X-ray goggles works best on a PC or Mac at the moment. However, once a webpage has been modified using X-ray Goggles, it can be saved (by creating a free account and logging in). The new modified and saved webpage will have a link, which can be visited by a tablet. Alternatively, the screenshots can be viewed on a tablet.

Keep calm and code

"Don't panic, don't panic!"

The 'Keep calm' posters are recognisable by their layout, font and the 'Keep calm and . . .' format. Get children to create their own and learn about coding too!

Can you create your own webpage? How would you introduce children to writing in the HTML language behind the webpage?

Following on from Idea 36, use the Mozilla Webmaker resources, focusing on their brilliant Thimble tool. Mozilla Thimble is a webpage, which shows the code on the left and the preview of the code on the right. If you go to the basic editor (thimble.webmaker.org/) it can look quite daunting, as it's almost blank. However, many volunteers at Mozilla have created a range of projects to help 'teach the web'.

A great starter project is to create a 'Keep Calm and Carry On' style poster. These posters follow a simple format that have been adapted by many people for different purposes. Using the Mozilla Thimble beginner project (bit.ly/100computing37) the children can see the code and begin to change the words on the poster. What will they want to do? They can use the 'Keep Calm and . . .' start and add their own words on the end. They can change the colour of the poster too.

Throughout the code in the left-hand panel, there are comments to help explain the function of each part. This means the children can continue the learning at home, where they can teach themselves using the example projects. The Thimble tool will work on tablet computers, though it currently works best on PC or Mac computers.

Teaching tip

Using the Zoom tool in the web browser can help to display parts of the screen and the code. If you want to draw the children's attention to part of the screen, using the CTRL (or CMD on a Mac) and the '+' key will zoom in. To zoom out again, use the CTRL and the '-' key.

Bonus idea ★

Ask the children to create posters for a school event or for the school rules. Once they have changed the text and the background colour, they can take a screenshot of the poster to display or share.

Make my 'meme'

"The Mozilla Thimble tool really helps to show how webpages are made."

Meme? What's a meme? It's a funny image, video or piece of text that spreads rapidly across the Internet, often being adapted as it goes. Using the fantastic Mozilla Thimble tool, the children can make their own.

In Idea 37, the children were introduced to Mozilla Thimble, the web-based tool which helps them learn about the structure of webpages.

Once the children have enjoyed playing with the Keep Calm project (Idea 37), they can try another, which encourages them to change the image, as well as the text. It's called Meme maker and is typical across the web, where an image or part of an image is replicated in different situations.

Now it's the children's turn to make a meme. They can begin by changing the text on an example of a cat. Using the Meme maker project (bit.ly/100computing38) let the children enjoy changing the captions.

The background image can be changed too. By using a Google image search (recommend using Safe Search primaryschoolict.com/) the children can find an image. Once selected, they can view the image; in the address bar of the web browser is the unique address of the image. They can copy and paste this address into the Thimble code.

Mozilla Thimble is a great learning tool. The children can reload the project to reset it, so if it stops working, they can start again. All the time they are experimenting they are learning how to code!

Paper prototyping

"Paper is an important tool in the digital world"

Quickly sketching or creating a paper prototype of the design for a webpage, game or app helps children to visualise how a series of buttons may be laid out and repeated on different pages.

Try the following:

- Explain to the children that they are going to make a mobile phone app. They need to decide what its purpose will be and how it will work. Using a simple storyboard format, ask them to sketch the screens of their app. For example, an emergency first aid app may have a home screen, which links to four screens for treating cuts, broken bones, scalds and burns. The home screen would need navigation to the other screens – what would it look like?

- Next, to show how the app may work, ask the children to create a paper prototype. They can draw the separate screens, cut them out and prepare to demonstrate their ideas. By talking through the paper prototype with a partner, they can see how it might perform.

- There is an example of paper prototying for a recipe app on YouTube here: bit. ly/100computing39.

The children enjoy making their paper prototype apps and it's great as a speaking and listening activity. Ask the children to video their paper prototypes and how they work when their partner tries it out. This process can be enlightening when the users see things in a different way to the app creator.

Tablet tip

There are apps which can add interactivity to paper prototypes. The POP app for iPad (popapp. in) enables the user to photograph their paper drawings and then add 'hotspot' areas to simulate buttons. Then the children can actually try out their app by navigating the separate screens, moving by pressing the parts of the image.

Taking it further

A professional tool for creating prototypes is called Balsamiq (balsamiq. com). It uses 'wireframes' or outlines of phones and tablets. It also has the buttons and components of apps, which can be added to make it look like a real app. Show the children the demo and they can try a desktop version to develop their ideas

Make me 'appy

"Making an app really excites the children."

The majority of children in your class will have seen and used apps on phones and tablets. Using Mozilla Appmaker they can make their own apps, including games. Components can be added and linked together. The apps can also be previewed live on phones.

Teaching tip

Before making apps, it's good to spend time looking at many examples of other apps. The Apps for Good (www.appsforgood.org/) organisation support schools to create apps through great resources, competitions and links to real businesses. Originally aimed at secondary schools, there are now upper primary schools becoming involved. Example winning apps can be viewed on their website (www.appsforgood.org/public/student-apps).

Tablet tip

There are tools to create and preview apps on tablets. Educational accounts are available for Appshed (appshed.com/academy/appshed-academy) or try a starter account to try it out. Also, AppFurnace (appfurnace.com/) will let you create apps which are then previewed on a phone or tablet, using the AppFurnace player app.

The Mozilla Webmaker tools are great ways of 'teaching the web'. In addition to X-ray Goggles and Thimble, they have developed Appmaker (apps.webmaker.org/designer) – a tool to create apps.

A good place to start is with an example project (webmaker.org/en-US/appmaker#starter-apps). Three example projects, Music app, Chat app and Fireworks app, are provided for the children to pull apart.

If the example apps look too complicated, then you can create a simple app:

- Using the blank template, press on the 'Button' brick in the left-hand side menu.
- On the app screen a button will appear saying 'Press me'.
- Now, from the left menu, select 'Fun' at the top and then the 'Fireworks' brick at the bottom.
- The Fireworks screen will appear on the phone.
- Now, when the button is pressed, a firework will fire across the screen.
- Let the children play with the different bricks and see what they can create.

There is a gallery of example apps created by volunteers: bit.ly/100computing40

Challenge the children to create a simple app, with three screens and buttons to navigate between them.

Minecraft

"Minecraft – endless digital LEGO!"

Minecraft is a very popular computer game for children in which they create objects and buildings. So, how could you use Minecraft in school?

Many children play Minecraft at home, on a PC, Xbox, Playstation or iPad, and they will often be working collaboratively to create buildings. Even at school, when the children have been asked to take out their reading books, they often read about Minecraft!

One way of using Minecraft in the classroom is to encourage the children to record videos of their worlds. For example, they could be learning about the Romans, so the children could recreate a Roman fort. Once complete, they can record screenshots or a video of their fort, explaining its construction and how it was used. This can be very empowering for the pupils, as they will be very proud of their creativity. Also, they will have to research Roman forts in order to create one. It is another way of giving us an insight into their understanding.

Geocraft is a great project, which is supported by the Ordnance Survey (www.geocraft.org.uk/what-is-geocraft). It combines real world maps with Minecraft to create a simulated world. The Geocraft project has begun to map parts of the UK which enables the children to build their locality. It helps them to engage in their environment and learn more about the geography and history of their local area. For example, children in Knutsford looked at their town and realised they needed to identify the landmarks, so they placed signposts in their Minecraft world. This links to digital literacy and teamwork skills.

Teaching tip

The Raspberry Pi minicomputer can enable the children to play Minecraft (pi.minecraft.net). A simple version, called Minecraft Pi, lets the children use the mini computer to build their worlds. The Raspberry Pi computers can be networked to enable collaboration too.

Tablet tip

There are some teachers who have begun to use Minecraft in schools, through the 'lite edition' – Minecraft LE, which is available on the iPad. This does not have the full functionality of Minecraft on the PC or Xbox, though it is still powerful enough to let the children make buildings and think spatially.

Banana piano

"Can you play a banana piano?"

How could you enable children to invent their own game controllers? A great tool called a MakeyMakey will let them become inventors.

Go to www.makeymakey.com and watch the introductory video. A MakeyMakey is a small board which attaches to a computer by a USB wire. Instead of pressing keys on the keyboard, you can attach different objects to control the computer. The video shows how bananas can become a piano keyboard, how a cat can take a selfie and how video game controllers can be made with Playdoh. The MakeyMakey works by forming an electrical circuit to 'press' the key.

One of the examples is a musical staircase. The 'Piano Stairs' video from The Fun Theory (www.thefuntheory.com) shows a staircase on a public transport station, where the stairs were converted into piano keys. Aluminum foil has been laid on the stairs and the wires attached.

Let the children play using the MakeyMakey attached to online video games which require a button to jump or move. The MakeyMakey video shows how to construct a game controller using saltdough buttons.

Another example is to use charcoal or a soft pencil to draw lines and shapes on paper. The wires from the MakeyMakey can be attached to the paper and the charcoal is able to conduct the electricity, so children can draw shapes, attach the wires and control the online computer games. The MakeyMakey can also be attached to the Scratch software. Children can create their own Scratch game and control it with a model. They could record their own voices, using the speech blocks, and activate phrases by using their controller.

Searching

Part 4

Hide and seek

"Use search technologies effectively."

The above is a quote from the National Curriculum. So, what do we mean by 'search technologies'? Let me Google that for you!

Looking for information online can be similar to a game of hide and seek. You may use a search engine, for example, Google, Bing, Yahoo or DuckDuckGo, but you will still need to help it look in the 'right' places. You may choose certain words that relate to your search or even type a whole question into the search box. Once the search results are displayed, you still need to read and evaluate them, to decide if they meet your needs.

- To get the children interested in searching accurately, use 'A Google a day' (agoogleaday.com). Each day a new challenge appears and the website states, 'There's no right way to solve it, but there's only one right answer.'
- Encourage the children to think of their own challenges for their friends to find, for example, 'What is the name of the first person to stand on the moon?' They would need to think of the search words to use, such as 'first man moon'. Let the children think of ten questions, swap with a partner, then they must find the answers (listing the search words they have used).
- To end the lesson, show the children a joke website called 'Let me Google that for you'. Think of a question and type it into the search box at www.lmgtfy.com. It creates a link, which when the preview button is pressed, shows an animation of itself typing the same question into Google, then shows the results, stating 'Was that so hard?'

Teaching tip

'Safe Search' (primaryschoolict.com) will search the websites, with some filters. No Internet filtering is perfect, but this at least gives some protection. With all use of the web, the children should know that they should always tell a trusted adult if they find content that upsets them.

Tablet tip

The Google app (also the Google search webpage) has integrated a voice search. Open the app and say 'OK, Google' and then say the words for your search. It will automatically search those words and display the results.

Taking it further

Ask the children to change their search questions from 'What was' or 'Who was' to 'Why was'. For example, 'Why was Neil Armstrong the first man on the moon?' This will now involve more reasoning, by firstly finding the facts and then adding their opinions or evidence from their searching.

Checking the facts

"... one last question."

When we search, we will often type in a couple of key words and look at the first and maybe second page of results. How can we conduct more effective searches? Introduce the 'Advanced search' tool on Google to students.

- Ask the children to search for the first man on the moon. Once they have their results, they can select the 'Cog wheel' icon, which produces a drop-down menu. From the menu, select 'Advanced search'. Now the search can be narrowed.
- The first options are 'Find pages with . . . ' and then choosing from 'all these words' or 'this exact word or phrase' or 'any of these words' or 'none of these words' or 'numbers ranging from'. This will help them to think about the words they have used and other ways to phrase the search question.
- The search can be narrowed by listing the results in any language or in any region, so that they could ask for only results in English. Another useful tool is to look for the 'last update' by selecting 'past 24 hours', 'past week', 'past month', 'past year' or 'anytime'. For a question about a current news story, they could find the latest updates.
- The 'reading level' option can filter the results based on an approximate reading age. If the 'annotate results with reading level' option is selected, the reading age will be displayed alongside the results, as basic, intermediate or advanced.
- Choose a theme for searching or link it to a current topic or lesson. Demonstrate the Advanced search and then see if the children can find more relevant results.

Teaching tip

A page can be searched by selecting 'Find' from the menu of the browser. For example, on the Neil Armstrong Wikipedia page the keyword of 'Eagle' can be found by selecting find and then the word 'Eagle'. A shortcut is to press the 'CTRL' key and the 'F' key on a Windows computer, or 'CMD' key and 'F' on a Mac. This can help the children find keywords on the pages they choose.

Taking it further

To learn more about searching, Google introduced a Powersearching course. One of the outcomes of the course was a very useful quick reference guide, which can be viewed at: www.powersearching withgoogle.com/course/ ps/assets/PowerSearching QuickReference.pdf. There is a search guide for children at: www. commonsensemedia.org/ blog/the-kids-guide-to-google-search.

That's rank

"Why is that the top result in your search?"

Who's top of the Premier league? Who's the best tennis player in the world? Who's number 1 in the charts? A quick search will let you know. How does the search know how to order the list of websites it finds? Could someone influence the order, so that their website appears higher in the search engine charts?

When a search using the Google search tool is carried out, how does Google know which result to place at the top? If researching a space topic and looking for Neil Armstrong, there could be over 31,000 results! The Wikipedia link appears near the top, so why is that?

To find out how search ranking works, you can do a search!

Alternatively, you could watch a simple introduction to how search ranking works by Matt Cutts of Google (bit.ly/100computing45a).

Google also have a whole section called 'How search works' (bit.ly/100computing45b). It shows that the first part is crawling and indexing the web. The second part is when someone searches using keywords, it searches Google's index of the websites it has found. It uses complex algorithms to decide which pages to select. They use over 200 factors to decide, including how many important pages link to that page. Finally, the third part is sorting out spam websites, to make sure the results are relevant.

Yes, and . . .

"Searching for answers is a really important skill."

Yeah, but, No, but, Yeah, but . . . when searching for answers we can make our searches more effective. In-between the keywords, we can use 'and' or 'not' to narrow the results. This is called 'Boolean logic' and we use it all the time.

To play the '20 questions' game, one person needs to think of an object and can only answer 'Yes' or 'No' to the other player, who tries to work out what the object is. It's a good starter to a search lesson, as the children need to think of appropriate questions and then refine them.

When using a search engine, the results are not as straightforward. The list of results can be refined by adding extra words or symbols. If two words are entered into a search, for example, 'Homer Simpson', then the results will look for 'Homer' AND 'Simpson', even though the word 'AND' was not added. A '+' could have been placed in-between the two words, to represent an 'AND'. To remove words, a minus sign '-' could be inserted. For example, 'Homer-Simpson'. So, the results will show all websites related to 'Homer' but not those related to Homer Simpson.

To demonstrate this to the class, ask them to stand up if they have a certain property, for example, if they have blue eyes, are right-handed and so on. The children stand up and sit down, depending on the answers. Then introduce an 'AND', for example, stand up if you like pizza and like Brussel sprouts. The 'NOT' or minus can be added: stand up if you have a pet and NOT a dog. Using 'AND' and 'NOT' is a way of introducing 'Boolean logic'; this is used by computers to process information through logic gates (inside its processor).

Teaching tip

When choosing features to select different children in the class, for example, eye colour or height, there are some times when you may need to be sensitive to their characteristics. Instead of choosing personal features, give the children pieces of coloured card, which have been cut into different shapes. Now, the instructions can be given 'Stand up if you have a yellow card' or 'Stand up if you have a yellow card AND it is a square' or 'Stand up if you have a yellow card that is NOT a triangle'.

Bonus idea ★

Fun paper-craft 'Logic goats' are available from www.robives.com/blog/logic_goats_set_four. When constructed, they represent 'Logic gates' in a computer. The AND goat will only nod its head when both the left and right buttons are pressed.

Let's go way back

"The problem with Internet quotes is knowing if they're true – Winston Churchill."

What was the web like when it first began? How has the Google page changed? If we wanted to find out about our local history, we could visit a museum or archive, but where do we go for ancient webpages?

Can you remember life before the World Wide Web? How did you find things out? How has the web changed?

The children in your class will not know life before the web, as it has always been around for them. It's good to show them how webpages have changed over the years. A useful tool for showing this is the 'Internet Archive' (archive.org/web/).

- Using the Internet Archive, choose a website which you use regularly with the children, for example, the BBC website. See how it has changed its design over the years. Display two examples to the children and see if they can guess which one is the oldest. Why do they think that?
- Let the children imagine a Google search page for ancient history, for example, what would it look like in Roman or Egyptian times. It's fun to imagine that we could look old-fashioned with our current webpages, in a few years' time.

Teaching tip

Trying to understand large periods of time can be difficult for the children, especially if it is before they were born. A website has a 'Search history' included, which shows the searches over time from the most recent to weeks, months or longer ago. Show the children the 'History' of the searches, so that they can see a search from that day, yesterday or last week. Prompt them to think about their 'digital footprint' as they walk across the web.

Tablet tip

Using the screenshot tool on a tablet allows the children to capture an image of the screen. Using the Internet Archive, ask them to capture three images of the Google search page, over time. Then use an app such as Shadow Puppet Edu to narrate over the images to describe the changes.

Staying safe

Part 5

Will you be my friend?

"What makes a good online friend?"

As a teacher and parent, I find I am always mediating between children and their friends. They seem to get on most of the time, they fall out, and then make friends again!

What are the characteristics of a best friend? Explore the following ideas:

- Ask the children to think of their friend and write five reasons why they are friends. Can they rank the five qualities in order from most important? Now, with a partner, do they agree on the qualities?
- Drawing a friend – using a large sheet of paper draw around one person. On to this outline figure ask the children to write the qualities that make a good friend. This makes a great display for the classroom, especially at the start of a year.
- Word cloud friends – using Wordle (www.wordle.net) or Tagxedo (www.tagxedo.com) enter the words that the children have suggested for a good friend. The words that are most frequent will appear larger than the other words. This also makes a great display.
- Once the children have decided what makes a good friend, ask them about friends online. This could be friends they have met face-to-face before or friends they have never met in person, but they would still consider to be friends. Do the qualities they identified before still count? Are online friends the same or different?

We want the children to realise that the qualities and behaviours of being kind and helpful friends when face-to-face should be the same as when online. Remind the children that if they feel upset by something online, they should tell a trusted adult.

Communicating online and offline

"Be kind, be specific, be helpful."

How do the children talk to each other? Are they kind? Would they talk differently if they were communicating online?

It is important for children to think about the words they say to each other. Give them five minutes to write as many kind words as they can remember. Now, give them five minutes to write unkind words. How many of each one did they write? Did they find it easier to think of unkind words?

When talking to their friends they need to use kind words. They would not use unkind words when talking face-to-face. What about if they were online? Would they behave differently?

Emphasise to the children that they need to behave the same towards each other whether face-to-face or online.

Online the children may communicate via messages (a chat room or email) or they might leave comments on a blog post. They may use video communication (such as Skype or FaceTime). One of the problems of not being face-to-face is that they may not pick up on visual clues and could misunderstand what a person means in a comment.

In the classroom, set up a video Skype call between two computers (one connected to a projector, so the class could watch). Ask one child to talk to the class via the video link. Do the children think it is the same as or different to being face-to-face?

Teaching tip

When the children are giving feedback to each other, the mantra should be 'Kind, specific and helpful'. For example, if one child gives a presentation and another gives feedback, their words should be kind. The advice to help them improve should be specific, for example, 'you could add an picture to help explain your idea'. Finally, the advice should be helpful, giving a positive message.

Taking it further

Ask the children to create a template for giving feedback. This could guide them when helping their classmates improve their work, when face-to-face. It could also remind them that they need to behave in a similar way when online, for example, commenting on a blog post.

Facefriend

"Who's got a Facebook account?"

Most children are aware of Facebook and many primary age children may even have an account. Are they allowed? What are the benefits and problems that may arise?

Make sure the children understand that they need to be 13 years old to have a Facebook or Twitter account. However, there may be online games or websites that they use which have social media aspects, so developing their knowledge of how to stay safe online, with the balanced view of the benefits, is very important.

If the children in your class do not have a profile on Facebook yet, they will probably have one here, or on another social networking site, in the future. Officially, they should be 13 years old, though some may have lied about their age to register.

Children need to think about how they represent themselves online and see both sides of social media – the benefits and how to be safe online. If you do not have a Facebook account, you should consider having one, simply to find out about it so you are in a better position to advise the children. You do not need to be active in posting comments but you can view other people's comments and see how it works. If you do have an account, it is worth reviewing your settings to see how you share your personal information. Also try the following resources:

- Facebook has an excellent 'Safety Centre' and Frequently Asked Questions to help people to stay safe (en-gb.facebook.com/safety).
- The Digitally Confident website is a great place to find advice (www.digitallyconfident.org). It tries to give a balanced view, showing the benefits of social media, as well as the issues which children and parents need to consider.
- The Digizen website has resources to support the benefits of social media (www.digizen. org/socialnetworking/benefits.aspx).
- The Thinkuknow website has resources to lead a class discussion about social media (www. thinkuknow.co.uk/8_10/control/social/).

Using sticky notes or the online sticky note tool Padlet.com, ask the children to write an idea relating to Facebook or social media. Then, together, sort the ideas into positive and negative aspects of social media.

Snappy chat

"Can you delete a message that has been shared online?"

What if someone sends you a message and then deletes it — has it really gone? Teach children the need to think before they share.

With SnapChat, the photo messaging tool, the user can text, send drawings, take photos and record videos, before sending to a list of recipients. However, these 'snaps' are time-limited and will disappear from the recipients' phones after a few seconds. The snaps are also deleted from SnapChat's servers. But have they really disappeared? We need the children to think about this, and even though they may not be using SnapChat or similar tools yet, you can prepare them.

Taking a screenshot on a computer, phone or tablet is very easy and quick to do. To show this, try playing the memory game!

- You have a hidden picture. In groups of four, the children take turns to see the picture for ten seconds. They return and describe it to the group, who try to redraw it. Continue until they have all had at least two turns.
- Look at the pictures drawn and show the original one.
- Now, with a new picture, repeat the process, but give one group a digital camera, so that they can photograph the hidden picture on their first go. The group with the camera can easily draw it, as they have the image saved on its screen.

Explain that this is like taking a screenshot. Just because SnapChat and other tools claim to remove the image, what is to stop a person taking a screenshot before it disappears? Also, others may have seen it and can describe what it looked like.

Teaching tip

Watch the e-safety video called 'Jigsaw' for eight to ten year olds (www.youtube.com/watch?v=_o8auwnJtqE) from CEOP (Child Exploitation and Online Protection Centre). It is quite a hard-hitting video about being careful about sharing online. It has a clear message and should be part of a balanced view, showing the benefits and positive aspects of being online, as well as the potential problems. Think about road safety; the children need to know the dangers, however, they should see the benefits to being outside and on the road.

Evacuees

"Is it safe?"

Where do children feel safe? Do they feel safe online? Can they move away from danger when they are online? Do they know whom to tell if they feel unsafe online? Using an 'evacuee' analogy, let's look at these questions.

Teaching tip

If preparing for a school inspection, sample questions from an inspector to the children could be:

1. If you felt uncomfortable about anything you saw, or if anybody asked you for your personal details such as your address, on the Internet would you know where to go for help?

2. If anybody sent you hurtful messages on the Internet or on your mobile phone would you know whom to tell?

3. Can you tell me one of the rules your school has for using the Internet?

4. Can you describe the risks of posting inappropriate content on the Internet?

It is important that the children can answer the questions, so that they are safe, and this also shows that you have put safety measures in place.

During World War II there was a wartime poster that had 'Children are safer in the country' as the main caption. Children had been evacuated from cities being bombed during the war to the countryside, for safety. However, when parents missed their children or they did not think the threat was as great as before, they began to bring the children back home. Hence the posters 'Children are safer in the country' began to appear. Is this similar for children online? Are there safer places? Can they move away from danger?

Ask the children to describe places where they feel safe. Are these places at home, school or somewhere else in the world? What makes them feel safe there? Can they describe a website they may use, which they know is safe?

When children are on the web, looking for images or information, guide them to safe places, such as known websites like the BBC. If they are to visit a particular website, you can check it before they go there. However, if they are searching, then there is a chance they may find something that upsets them or makes them feel uncomfortable. When they are at school, there is often web filtering set up to try to catch unpleasant content, but this may not be the case when the children are at home. Therefore, you need to explain what they should do.

For e-safety, the statements relating to reporting concerns in the National Curriculum document are:

- For Key Stage 1: identify where to go for help and support when they have concerns about content or contact on the Internet or other online technologies.
- For Key Stage 2: identify a range of ways to report concerns about content and contact.

The statements both say that the children should tell someone, whether that is to go and tell them face-to-face or, with Key Stage 2, know other ways of reporting their concerns. The following ideas may help:

- For younger children, you could try the Hector the Protector's safety button, which is a downloadable tool (hectorsworld.netsafe. org.nz/teachers/hectors-world-safety-button). If the children see something on the screen that they don't like, then they press the button and the screen is filled with a dolphin screensaver. They can then go and tell their teacher or trusted adult. An alternative is simply switching off the screen, via the power button.
- Older children could report concerns by emailing a named person at school. Also, the CEOP has a report button, which children can use to contact them about concerns (www.ceop.police.uk/safety-centre).
- Using the evacuees theme, ask the children to pretend to be children being moved away from danger. They need to know who to tell if they feel worried. Evacuees also carried a gas mask to protect them – the gas mask made it harder to see, so the analogy could be, if you do not like what you see put your mask on (the Hector screensaver, closing your eyes or turning the screen off).

Tablet tip

Using an app such as Morfo (it animates faces from photographs) ask the children to find images of evacuees and record their own voices giving e-safety advice. They could continue the analogy between evacuees and staying safe, for example, they could describe how the evacuee moved away from danger and then explain that if they find something upsetting online, they should move away from it and tell an adult.

Taking it further

For further advice on e-safety, visit the Digitally Confident website (digitallyconfident.org), where there is practical advice separated into sections for 'Children', 'Adults who work with young children' and 'Parents and carers'.

Life-logging

"Imagine if your whole life was recorded as a video!"

What is a 'digital footprint'? What information is collected or shared when the children go online?

Ask children to think about their lives to date. What have been the most significant parts or key milestones? Link this to history and creating timelines. Try the following ideas:

- Create a photo album for the major points in their lives and ask the children to sketch pictures to represent the moments (instead of using real photos).
- Now, ask them to imagine that these special days had been recorded as a video. For example, some cyclists can now have a camera to video their journeys, in case of an accident. Most days, it may be a simple 'forgettable' journey, but one day it could be vital that they recorded the events.
- Can the children think of all of the things they did on that special day and decide what would be the most important parts? Then, using digital cameras, ask them to recreate the important scenes, either as still images or as a video. Let them present their events to the class and explain why they are significant.
- Ask the children to think about what they might like to do as a job when they complete their education. Can they imagine their lives in the future and choose five significant events? Using the camera, ask them to act out the scenes for their 'life log'.
- Save the life logs for the future, like a time capsule, so the children can look back and see what they imagined would happen.

Pirates ahoy!

"What would an imaginary pirate have on their social media profile?"

How do you know if you're a pirate . . . you just arrrrre! The children will know about pirates, at least the stereotypical pirate with eye patch, wooden leg, hook, parrot and gold. A quick, fun idea is to make a pirate profile.

When thinking about profiles, what pieces of information do we need to include? If it was for the school records, then lots of information: name, surname, date of birth, address, parent or carer details, medical information. However, for a children's online game or website the pupils need to think carefully about what they share. Also, they want to share a little about their interests and hobbies, so that others may see what interests them. Considering this now is good preparation for when they are older and sharing on social media.

Using a pirate example really gets the children interested. They can create a profile for a pirate, thinking about what they should include:

- Name: in full or just first name and initials?
- Age: do they need to share their date of birth or can they just add an age?
- Location: do they need to give their address or will an approximate location do?
- Interests: do they need to give the times and places where they do their clubs, hobbies or interests or can they simply list the general types of things they like?
- Photograph: do they use an avatar (a cartoon representation) or a real photo?

For their imaginary pirate, the children can create the social media profile, then discuss in pairs the information they have given. Does their pirate sound interesting, while still protecting sensitive information?

Teaching tip

The pirate social media profiles can make a colourful display. Once the children have considered the pirate, they can make their own profiles for themselves. Are they comfortable for their profiles to be displayed to the school? If they feel uncomfortable, why? Is it because they feel they are sharing too much about themselves? Help them feel in control, so that if they want to change the information, they can, or if they decide to not display their profiles, then that is fine too.

Tablet tip

Using Fakebook (www. classtools.net/FB/home-page), ask the children to create a false profile for their pirate or themselves. This can be used for many purposes, for example, a famous explorer in history, or an influential scientist in science.

p4ssW0rd

"Is your password secure? Can it be easily guessed?"

It would astound you to know how many people use the word 'password' for their password. How can we improve the strength of the passwords and why would we want to?

We use passwords for many different situations. You will have one for many things from your email to your online bank account and children will also begin to have them as they get older – all need good passwords.

Ask one child to choose a password. It should be something personal to them. The other children have to try to guess the password. Can they? Do they know something about the child that would give them a clue about their password choice?

Often people chose simple words, such as a favourite colour or surname. We need to think about making the passwords more secure.

For fun, show the children the 'Passive Aggressive Password Machine' (www.trypap. com). Type in a password and it makes a comment, relating to its strength, for example, 'toddlers eat passwords like yours, for breakfast'.

A great tip from Simon Finch (@simfin), who advises schools on e-safety, is to think of a sentence about something the children like, then select the first letter from each word, then change some letters for numbers or lower case.

For example, 'I love watching football on TV':

1. Take the first letter from each word – ILWFOT
2. Change some letters for numbers – ILWF0T
3. Change some capitals for lower case – ILWF0t

By using a sentence, it is harder to forget the word or where capitals or numbers were used.

Spam, spam, spam

"Spam is a funny word, but spam emails may not be so funny."

Can the children describe 'spam'? Spam can mean unwanted emails or messages that appear. These messages can be disguised to look like they are from people or organisations you know. The children need to know how to spot spam!

Spam messages can be very frustrating. They can offer products at low prices, prizes or money. To the children, this will seem very tempting, so they need to learn to spot spam! Get the children to make up some example spam email titles. This could be 'You've won a prize!' or 'iPads for £25'. Do they sound too good to be true?

Explain that the sender's email address will also give a clue that it is spam:

- Has the email come from someone you know?
- Does it look official?
- Have you entered a competition or signed up to a mailing list recently, which looks like it is connected to the email address?

Warn the children that sometimes spam emails have a link or an attachment on them, which will install a virus on the computer. If they think it is spam, they must not open it!

Mailing lists and competitions often have check boxes at the bottom, which may say 'Do you want to receive emails from our partners?' Sometimes, these can be tricky and say 'If you do not want to receive emails, then tick the box'. Explain that they need to watch out for these messages.

Finally, encourage the children to use a spam filter. Many email accounts will have a basic filter on to try to stop some spam emails coming through. Ask the children to check with their parents whether they have anti-virus and spam filters and also that they are up-to-date.

Teaching tip

Keep a glossary of terms to help the children understand the new words they come across. Make a display of these words with a simple definition next to them.

Bonus idea ★

Play the Yes/No game to show the children how they need to think carefully when ticking boxes to say yes or no to terms and conditions or receiving emails from people. One person tries to make a partner say the words 'Yes' or 'No', by asking questions such as 'Are you a boy?' 'Do you go to this school?' If they say yes or no then swap over and see who can win the most number of times.

Twitter for teachers

"#learning #teaching #sharing"

Twitter has changed my life. It has connected me to many other teachers, sharing great ideas. It took a while to overcome my scepticism and to begin to find it useful, but now I've started, it has really helped develop my teaching. How can you start or continue to develop your network?

Teaching tip

Every time I visit Twitter, I find new ideas. Here's a list of 25 pedagogical ideas, which people found through sharing on Twitter (ukedchat. com/2014/12/19/25-pedagogy-ideas-that-teachers-found-on-twitter/). It takes time to develop a network of teachers, similar to starting at a new school, you need time to meet people. Have a look at the list of 101 teachers to follow on Twitter that @teachertoolkit recommends. You will then start to see what others are saying and can follow them too. Twitter is the best professional development I have ever had.

We all have networks. Whether it's a network of family, friends or work colleagues, we communicate and connect with them all in different ways and for different things. When you are at school, you will know whom to ask about different subjects or lesson resources. You may have been to a conference or course, where you have met someone who is teaching a similar subject and they share their ideas. Imagine if you could stay connected with them or even connect with other teachers, sharing resources?

Twitter is a social network site on which people communicate in short messages of 140 characters. There are many famous celebrities who use Twitter, for example, Stephen Fry and Taylor Swift. People think that using 140 characters is making the language simpler, but actually to get a message across, you need to think carefully about the information to share and how to communicate it clearly.

Another misconception is that Twitter is simply used to share trivial information. It can in fact be a powerful tool to connect and share information between teachers. Think of it like the staff room – the majority of talk will be about lessons and school events, but there is social information mixed in.

Twitter can be used to pass information, for example, a link to a person's blog post about teaching, an announcement about an educational event or a link to a useful website for teaching computing.

'Have you seen the Barefoot computing resources? Just tried out Scratch fossil activity. Great for primary schools http://barefootcas.org.uk'

Get started with Twitter today! Create an account and watch the messages that other people are sharing. This will give you an insight into the type of content being shared. However, you need to know which other teachers to listen to or 'follow'. I'd recommend that you add a profile picture (it can be an object or cartoon if you do not feel comfortable about adding a photo of yourself) and complete the short profile about yourself. This might be simply: Teacher, just starting with Twitter, interested to find out how it will support learning.

Organisations such as the TES (@tes) and the Guardian Education (@GuardianEdu) have Twitter accounts, which have regular updates on educational matters and current teaching news.

'Bring a teacher to Twitter' is a great idea to help teachers get started. Basically, teachers already using it share why they find it useful. Look at the posts on the blog page to learn more: https://batttuk.wordpress.com/.

Twitter can also be used to have discussions. A hashtag is a short word or series of words to identify a topic and a good example is #ukedchat. Each week, on Thursday between 8–9 pm, teachers discuss an educational topic. Try searching for #ukedchat and see the messages being shared.

Twitter can be used with the children (keeping in mind that the Twitter account needs to be owned by a person over 13 years old). You can have an account for your class and the children could either write the tweets on paper for you to post or type them out to post with your approval. The tweets could be sharing what the children have been doing in the lessons or when they have been on a visit out of school.

Tablet tip

Using the Twitter app is easier than accessing Twitter via a webpage. Other Twitter apps, such as Tweetdeck, enable columns to be added for different people, so you can easily see what they are sharing.

Bonus idea

The concept of condensing a conversation into 140 characters is a fun activity to try with the children. Can they still get their point across in 140 characters? If they write three sentences about their hobbies, then edit them to reduce the characters to 140, which words do they remove? Another fun activity is to try to describe a film less than 140 characters, for example, 'Girl in a house is swept away in a hurricane & lands on a witch. She meets a scarecrow, tin man and lion and gets home, along a yellow road'

How do computers work?

Part 6

Build your own computer

"Steve Jobs built a computer – now it's your turn."

Making computers out of cardboard boxes is tremendous fun. The children really enjoy making their own computers and they learn about the components and their functions too.

Children enjoy making models using cereal packets, yoghurt pots and string. We can use this enthusiasm to learn about computers.

Ask the children to secretly sketch a model of a computer, and then show a partner. Do they look similar? They might imagine it looks like a desktop computer or a laptop. They may even have drawn a tablet computer. Most likely, they sketch a large desktop computer, which may be like the ones at school.

Now explain that they can 'make' their computer using cardboard and other materials. Let the children decide what they are going to make and how they are going to construct it. Tell them that once complete they will present their computer to the class and so will need to know the names of the component parts. The basic parts which they need to know are:

- screen
- keyboard
- mouse
- printer
- speakers
- the main 'thinking' part – depending on their understanding; you may call it the 'main box where it does the working out' or the 'processor' (for older children the 'Central Processing Unit' or CPU).

Let the children experiment with making their computers and then have a 'show and tell' session, to display the parts and name them. Can they explain the purpose of each part?

Hunting for wires

"We're going on a wire hunt. I'm not scared."

There are many electrical objects that the children see every day in school. They may take them for granted and not realise that they need to be plugged in to work. So, let's go on a wire hunt!

It is easy not to notice all the electrical items around us, as they are so familiar and integral to our lives these days. Get children to identify electrical everyday objects so that they can begin to recognise which ones have computers inside them. Then get them to consider how the computers make different objects work and which objects need to connect to the Internet to share or gather information. Try the following:

- Younger children (Key Stage 1): take them on a 'wire hunt' – looking around the school, which objects can they find which have wires? For example, a photocopier, telephone, TV, projector, computer.
- Children in lower Key Stage 2: challenge them to look for objects with wires and consider which ones might have computer processors inside. Take them to visit a local supermarket or museum to hunt for wires.
- Children in upper Key Stage 2: encourage them to think about which objects connect to the Internet. More and more objects use the Internet to be controlled by phones or computers, for example, house thermostats or plug sockets. This can be referred to as the 'Internet of Things' (en.wikipedia.org/wiki/Internet_of_Things) and it will become more important to the children in the future (see Idea 66).

Teaching tip

When the children are hunting for wires, they can work individually, in pairs or small groups. For the older children, when working in small groups, give roles to each child: timer (keeps the group moving and completing the hunt by a certain time); list manager (who either writes the list or checks items off a list); photographer (who captures the images); observer (who observes how well the group works together and feeds back to the class on their performance).

Tablet tip

The Book Creator app enables the children to collate their images and add text or voice recordings. Ask the children to share their books or combine them into a larger 'Hunting for wires' class book. Alternatively, you can create a template book and share that with the groups, to guide them, as they look for the technology around them.

How are we connected?

"How does our computer magically connect to the Internet?"

How do wireless computers, tablets and phones know what is going on? Children may not think about how their computer connects to the Internet. They may have heard adults say, 'I can't get a phone signal' or 'The computer has lost the Wi-Fi' — so, what does this mean?

Start by playing 'Whispers' — the children sit in a circle and one person whispers a sentence in their neighbour's ear. They then pass the message to the next person and so on, until it returns to the original whisperer. Has the message changed? How could they make sure the message would not change? The information has been passed over a distance from one place to another.

Think about how people have sent information over a distance in the past — semaphore, smoke signals, flashing lights with Morse code. Let the children research different messaging systems and let them try sending a message from one end of the school yard or field to the other.

Now tell them to think about computers, and how the information is sent over a long distance, either using wires or wirelessly. To demonstrate sending information via wires, ask the children to make 'paper cup telephones' — where they connect two paper cups or tins via a length of string. When the string is taut, they can hear each other speaking.

Finally, to demonstrate wireless technologies, talk to the children about radios (if possible show them a radio using batteries, so it can show how the music plays without any wires). Tell the children about how a computer can be connected to another by sending the information wirelessly. To demonstrate use the website 'A web whiteboard app' on two wireless computers:

- Visit the webpage: awwapp.com.
- Select 'Start drawing'.
- Select 'Menu' and 'Invite' and it will give you an address to type into the second computer.
- Type the address into the second computer and then you should see the shared whiteboard.
- Ask one child to draw on one computer and the picture should appear on the other one and vice versa.

Explain that the information could be travelling a very long way: from the computer to the network point in the classroom, to a network hub in the school, to another computer and then many other computers, to the web whiteboard app, and then all the way back again!

Tablet tip

The web whiteboard app will work with tablet computers and there are a number of collaborative apps for drawing, for example the BaiBoard app allows pictures to be uploaded and then annotated, collaboratively.

Bonus idea ★

Ask the children to make a map of the school and then label the network points and the wired network computers. Is there a big server computer in the school? Add it to the map!

Mind the gap

"The London Tube map is a great example of a network. We can use it to describe computer networks too."

Computer networks may sound confusing, but they are similar to train networks. Stand clear of the doors, please!

Show children the National Rail map (www.nationalrail.co.uk/css/ OfficialNationalRailmaplarge.pdf), pointing out the names of places and how you get from A to B following the network lines. Ask the children to choose two places and to explain how they would get from one to the other. Make the analogy that if you wanted to send information from a computer from the first to second place, it would need to follow a network too. You can do the same with the London Underground map: (www.tfl.gov.uk/maps/track).

What would happen if a station was blocked? Ask the children to choose two places and describe their route, but then select a station along their chosen route and say it is blocked. Can they find another way around?

Computer networks are similar. Data moves from one place to another by computers passing it along their network. When there is a blockage, the computers pass the data to other computers, so that the data still arrives at its destination, but may take a different route. So, if one computer enters a search word into a Google search webpage, then the data is passed from computer to computer until it arrives at the Google computers, then the reply will go back, via many computers, to the person searching. All of this happens very quickly. Try it yourself; search for a keyword and, at the top of the Google result page, it will say how many results and how long it took to find them (often less than a second!).

Taking it further

Fantastic resources and help can be found on the Computing at School (CAS) website. Mark Dorling has shared his teaching ideas on 'Networks unplugged', which explain networks in a greater depth and also using paper-based resources (community. computingatschool.org. uk/resources/2528).

What's the address?

"You've got mail! The children realised that information is delivered to their computer's address."

Ask the children for their address and they should be able to tell you. It may follow a format of house name or number, street name, town name and postcode. Computers have addresses and a certain format too.

In the book *The Jolly Postman* by Janet and Allan Ahlberg the postman knew the addresses he was delivering to. Tell the children that when computers connect to the Internet, they need an address too. In a similar way to the postman needing an address to deliver letters so that people receive information, the computers need an address to receive information.

Each computer will have an 'IP address' – this is an 'Internet Protocol address', which allows the computer to be identified. You can read more about IP addresses on the Google help pages. When you search using Google's search tool, it tags your request with your IP address, so that once it has an answer it knows where to send the information.

To find out your computer's IP address, in the Google search box, type, "what is my ip". It will return a series of numbers, separated by points, for example, 82.39.63.201.

The IP address can also show an approximate location in the world. This can help with location services, such as weather reports. Try typing 'weather' into a Google search box and it should show you the weather where you are.

In Idea 63, Pinging packets, we will look at how the information is sent and received by computers.

Teaching tip

Highlight to the children the need to be safe online. Explain that the IP address can identify a computer, so that every search they do on the web can be traced back to it. When the children search for their IP address, they are shown the public address, so they may all seem to get the same numbers. However, inside the school, each computer will be given an internal or private address. Therefore, they should always carefully consider the words and subjects they search for, as it can be tracked online.

Pinging packets

"Time for a special delivery!"

Think about emails, webpages, images — they all contain data, so how do we send data from one computer to another?

Imagine you have an enormous dinosaur skeleton. It needs to be delivered to a museum in another country — how will you send it? Ask children this question and they may have many ingenious ideas. One idea could be breaking the skeleton into individual bones, labelling them and sending them by post. In this case, the person putting it back together would need instructions to construct the skeleton correctly. They would also need to know how many parcels to expect, so that they know that none of them are missing. Sending data via the Internet is similar.

On the Internet, every webpage and email is sent and received as 'packets of data'. When an email is sent, the network breaks it into parts of a certain size (called a 'packet'). The packet contains the sender's address, the recipient's address, the total number of packets and the number of that individual packet. The packets are sent by the best route, so that they can get to their destination quickly and efficiently. Also, if there is a blockage on that route, the packets can go another way. All of the packets are brought together on the destination computer to form the webpage or email. Try the following games to demonstrate packets of data:

- Start with a simple jigsaw. Give the pieces to one child to construct the picture. Then say 'Go' and at the other end of the classroom, another child will reconstruct the same jigsaw, but the pieces need to be passed to them. So, the first child breaks off a piece of the complete puzzle and passes it to a child, then another piece to another child and so on. The idea is that the pieces can travel in different directions to arrive at their destination. When complete, ask the child who received the jigsaw about their experience. They will probably say they did not know how many pieces were coming.

- Cut up a picture into 20 pieces and on the back of each write a number, from one to 20 (each piece has a different number). Now, under the writing of the number add the words 'of 20 pieces' or write 1/20, 2/20, 3/20, for example. Repeat the previous game and see if it is now easier to complete, because they now know there will be 20 pieces coming. However, the child reconstructing the picture will not know what it looks like, so they may say that having the extra information of the original picture would help them reconstruct it.
- Now let the children decide on a system of numbering the pieces, for example, numbering one to five across the top row, then six to ten on the next. They are deciding upon a 'protocol' or way of organising the information. Once the person reconstructing the picture knows how many pieces are coming and how to put them together, it should be much easier, faster and more accurate.

Explain that all webpages, emails and other information are sent via the Internet as packets of information, but a protocol is needed so that it can be sent and received accurately by the computers.

Taking it further

The children could research to find out what 'HTTP' means?
Why does it appear at the start of a web address?
Who invented it?

Bonus idea ★

The children could invent their own story about packets being delivered. For example, the book *The Jolly Postman* is about a postman visiting different characters and delivering items. Could the children write a story about the journey of the packets around the world and then ending up at a fictional character's house to be reconstructed into a webpage or picture? Could there be an incident in the story, so that the packets have to take an alternative route?

When I'm 64

"2, 4, 8, 16, 32, 64"

When my father was buying his first computer, I said 'Get a 120 MB hard drive, you'll never fill that!' Nowadays, you may struggle to find a USB pen drive that small.

Computers are getting faster, more accurate and smaller every day. A great way to think about the changes in technology is the acronym SCARF!

S: smaller
C: cheaper
A: accurate
R: reliable
F: faster

Ask the children to think about phones, computers or any other technology in their lives. How has it changed (using SCARF)? How will it change in the next five years? Is there a limit to how small things can be? Could phones be too small for our hands? What do they think the technology will be like when they are 64?

Give the example of the memory size inside our computers. As they are based on the binary system for storing the information, computer memory can follow the doubling pattern, for example, 1, 2, 4, 8, 16, 32, 64, 128. Currently, many iPhones or iPads may come in memory storage sizes of 16 GB, 32 GB, 64 GB or 128 GB (where GB stands for gigabytes of memory). These sizes are huge compared to a few years ago, as the larger memory was expensive, large, less accurate, less reliable and not fast. As technology moves on, so will the familiar memory sizes the children will see for phones and tablets.

Taking it further

Moore's Law is a computing term, which states that computer processor speeds or computing power will double every two years. It may not be a precise rule, but it indicates how computers are improving rapidly with time. For computer science, it is important that the children are aware of Moore's Law, though the main teaching point is that technology is changing rapidly.

Bonus idea ★

Let the children cut up a catalogue and collect pictures of technology. Can they see the numbers and predict how the items will change in the future, using SCARF?

Tim who?

"Who invented the web?"

Do you know who invented the World Wide Web? Do the children? Remember: the web has been in existence throughout their whole lifetimes, along with the concept of searching online to 'Google' something.

For primary children, the web has always been around, but do they know how it was invented? Which key words would they use to search to find out about this?

Tim Berners-Lee is the man who is accredited with inventing the World Wide Web. Challenge the children to find out about him and his story. One possible source is on the BBC History website (bit.ly/100computing65b).

On Tim Berners-Lee's own website he has 'Answers for young people', which respond to a number of questions about how he invented it (www.w3.org/People/Berners-Lee/Kids.html).

Hang on a minute? Are we talking about the Internet or the World Wide Web? Is there a difference? We often use the words interchangeably, so what could be the difference? (bit.ly/100computing65c).

The Internet is the physical network of computers and wires, but the World Wide Web is the software that runs on the computers, to enable communication. More simply the Internet connects computers, the web connects people.

Ask the children to make a display to explain the difference or even an interactive animation using the Scratch software.

Teaching tip

To develop your own knowledge about Tim Berners-Lee, watch his TED Talk 'The next web' (bit.ly/100computing65a). He explains how data and the relationships between data are a huge part of our lives and will become more important in the future.

Tablet tip

Using the facial animation app, Morfo, the children could use an image of Tim Berners-Lee to tell his story and, crucially, the difference between the Internet and the web.

The Internet of Things

"What is 'The Internet of Things'?

More and more devices are connecting together. For example, the smoke detectors in a house could be connected to the internet, so if you were not in your house and a fire began, it could alert you on your phone and call the Fire Brigade. What else do you think could be connected?

Teaching tip

Keep the conversation balanced with the benefits and potential problems of the Internet of Things. We want the children to be inspired at how technology can make our lives better, while making them aware of the information that is currently shared about themselves and how more could be shared in the future. We want them to feel in control of their personal information.

Taking it further

Ask the children to investigate 'driverless cars'. Would it be safer, for example, if the driver fell asleep or had a heart problem? Learn about 'How do driverless cars work' using the information and video on the Telegraph website www.telegraph.co.uk/motoring/motoringvideo/11308777/How-do-driverless-cars-work.html).

Show the children the YouTube videos 'The Internet of Everything Possibilities' (bit.ly/100computing66a) and 'Internet of things will change everything – including ourselves' (bit.ly/100computing66b).

The Internet of Things (IoT) is the network of physical objects that contain embedded technology to communicate and interact with their internal states or the external environment (according to Gartner's glossary bit.ly/100computing66c).

It seems amazing how more technology could connect together to change our lives. How do the children imagine this could be used in schools? How would their location be useful to automate activities? Could they order their school dinner to be ready as they walk into the dining hall?

Is there a negative side to people always knowing where you are? Talk to the children about which pieces of information they are happy to share? What do they already share? For example, an iPhone has a 'Find my phone' feature, so the phone can be found if it is lost or stolen. What if someone the children did not know gained access to the information, would that worry them? How do they know the information about them which is held by a company is safe?

Again, but slower

"Wikipedia can explain things, but is there a simpler way?"

'Please could you say that again, but slower?' Wikipedia contains a huge amount of information but sometimes I need a simpler version, thank goodness for the Simple English Wikipedia!

Wikipedia is 'the free encyclopedia that anyone can edit'. When the children search for something, the Wikipedia article will be near the top of the results. There are benefits to Wikipedia, for example, expert or local knowledge can be added, making the description of a place more accurate. However, a disadvantage is that inaccurate information could also be added. Therefore, it is important to stress to the children that Wikipedia is one source of information and they need to confirm the facts, using other references.

There are different language versions of Wikipedia (meta.wikimedia.org/wiki/List_of_Wikipedias), including a Simple English Wikipedia, which has simpler words and grammar (simple.wikipedia.org). Try choosing a few articles and see if the language is more accessible to your class. A useful exercise is to compare the main Wikipedia page with the Simple Wikipedia page. For example, search for the page on 'Neil Armstrong' on one, then open a new window and look at them together. Hopefully, the children can see there is less text on the simple version and also simpler sentences. Has any important information been removed?

A great way of comparing the pages is to use 'Again, but slower' – a special website, which places the two articles side-by-side (oranchak. com/againbutslower/). Would our lessons benefit from being 'Again, but slower'? What language and grammar do we use and is it accessible for the children?

Taking it further

Inside the Apple accessibility features on a Mac there is a 'Summarise Service'. Highlight text on a Wikipedia page and, from the browser menu, select 'Services' then 'Summarise'. You can then summarise text in a certain number of words or paragraphs. What are the pieces of information or words that are removed?

Bonus idea ★

Create a Wikipedia book! In the menu on the left-hand side of the Wikipedia page, select 'Print/Export'>'Make a book', then press 'Start Book Creator'. Search for pages to add to your book and, in the new menu at the top of the page, select 'Add this page to your book'. Once you have collected a few pages, select 'Show book'. Give it a title and subtitle, then download your book as a PDF document. All the information is in one document, which could be used offline or to focus your children on a particular article.

Data, data, data

Part 7

What's in a name?

"Let's decode the computing words."

'Use technology purposefully to create, organise, store, manipulate and retrieve digital content' (National Curriculum for computing). When using computers, we do all these things, but maybe use different words to describe what we are doing.

We are identified by our names and so are different files on the computer. There are two parts to naming files: one is choosing a suitable file name, the other is the file format.

File names and folders which are named appropriately are easier to retrieve. One child named a file '123' because it was easy to type, but in the next lesson they were not sure which file they needed. An appropriate file name is also important when sharing files with other people, so they know what it may contain. They can be simple names, but the aim is that the children or someone else could infer what the file contained just by looking at the name.

The file extensions describe the types of digital content: a 'jpg' is an image file, a 'doc' is a word processing file (for Microsoft Word), 'mov' or 'mp4' are video files and an 'mp3' is an audio file. It is important for the children to recognise these common file types and be able to describe the type of digital content.

So, to relate back to the National Curriculum statement, the files the children save are digital content that they are storing. They then retrieve the files when they go and find the file to load. Moving files into named folders can be described as organising digital content. An example of manipulating digital content could be editing a photograph to enhance it or cropping the image.

Teaching tip

A glossary of words is a great way for the children to decipher computing terms. Ask them to keep a list in a word processor file or as a presentation, with each word and a definition on separate slides.

Tablet tip

When using a tablet it can be more difficult to see the file type, for example, when a photo is taken, it goes into the 'Photos' or 'Camera Roll'. However, there are many opportunities for creating, manipulating and retrieving digital content when taking photos, adjusting them in photo apps and then retrieving them for different purposes in other apps.

Vote now!

"Voting opens now!"

It's voting time! The National Curriculum states that the children should be 'collecting, analysing, evaluating and presenting data and information'. How can they collect data? Can technology help us?

In your classroom there are many ways to gather information. You can:

- Take a quick vote by asking children to put their hands up.
- Ask if the children understand something by putting their thumbs up (if they are sure), thumbs down (if they are definitely not sure) and thumbs on the side (if they are not completely sure).
- Ask children to vote by clapping and the loudest clap wins.
- Ask children to write their answer on a drywipe board.
- Ask the children to write votes on a piece of paper and count the number of votes.
- Label the four corners of a room and ask the children to stand in one to show their opinion.

If you were to use the same method every lesson, it would become boring, so it is likely that you choose from a range of approaches for the most appropriate and also to vary the learning experience.

We can gather information digitally too. You may have used voting pads in the past, where the children could select an answer A, B, C, D, E or F, for example. These often took a long time to set up and the pads were expensive, so had limited success in the classroom.

New voting tools have become available which take advantage of our current technology.

A free web tool called Socrative enables any device which can access the web to be used (socrative.com/). Try the following:

- When first visiting the Socrative website, there a helpful video you can watch. You can create a free account, which then gives you a room number. Login as the teacher and ask the children to login as the 'Student' and enter your room number.
- From your teacher dashboard, select 'Quick Quiz.' Now you can ask your children a question and get feedback straight away (without having to spend time preparing the quiz before the lesson). For example, a true/false question could be: 'Wales is larger than Scotland, true or false?' A multiple-choice question could be: 'Do you understand what you need to do for your homework? A for definitely know what to do, E for no idea what to do or B, C or D for somewhere in-between'.
- The 'Short answer' quick quiz question tool is very useful. It enables the children to enter text and then vote on the answers. For example, it could be: 'What is the most important factor in healthy eating?' or 'If you could give one piece of advice for staying safe online, what would it be?' The children can type their advice into the answer box and, when complete, all of the answers can be shared with the class and they can vote upon them, to choose the most important. A simpler use would be to vote for someone to be a class representative – each of the candidate's names could be added and then voted upon. When finished the results can be viewed or sent as an attachment to the teacher (the results are in the form of a spreadsheet).

Get your fingers ready – it's time to vote!

Kangaroo court

"You cannot be serious? I'm voting against that!"

'That's ridiculous!' said one child in my class. 'How can they possibly get away with that?' We looked at a real court case and used voting tools to make decisions throughout our recreated trial.

Teaching tip

Each quiz that is created has a special identifying number (a SOC quiz number). This means that you can share quizzes between teachers, for example, if you created a baseline maths quiz, you can share it with another teacher, who can run it with their class. There are shared quizzes to try at garden.socrative.com/.

Taking it further

Ask the children to create their own quizzes. They can have their own Socrative accounts, if they are given permission by a parent or carer. An alternate method for creating the quizzes is to use the spreadsheet template (which can be downloaded from Socrative). The children could create questions and add them to the template. You could then import their quiz into your list of Socrative quizzes and run it with the class. (To do this, from the Dashboard, select 'Manage quizzes' and 'Import a Socrative quiz using an Excel file').

In Idea 69, Vote now! we talked about using quick questions with voting pads. I suggested using the web-based Socrative tool. One example of pre-prepared questions that I've used with a class is 'Kangaroo Court'. We looked at a court case and after each piece of evidence the class voted on whether to side with or against the person bringing a complaint.

The case was one about a lady who bought a coffee from a McDonalds in America. While sitting in the car, she opened the lid on the coffee and spilt it over herself. She needed hospital treatment and was ill for a long time. She went on to sue McDonalds for the coffee being too hot: (bit.ly/100computing70). We broke the case into smaller chunks. Each question in Socrative presented a little more of the case and asked the children which side they would vote for and they could also add some text to explain their answer.

The children really enjoyed using the voting tools, because they could instantly see the results and how the class was voting.

At the end of a lesson, the 'Exit ticket' tool is used to gather information about the learning. The children can answer the questions about the lesson on multiple devices, or even one device which is passed around the class. The questions could be based upon the lesson objectives or on the bigger picture of the learning over the topic.

Emotion graphs

"The children loved thinking about the emotions of the characters and explaining their graphs."

Pharell Williams' song *Happy* describes him being happy, 'like a room without a roof'. However, if he was sad, would he be 'like a room without a floor'? The idea of emotions going up and down can relate to emotion graphs. We can plot the emotions of characters throughout a story.

Think of a fairy tale, such as *Little Red Riding Hood*. Her emotions change throughout the story, going up and down. Use this to engage the children in plotting graphs of emotions. Choose major points (a maximum of ten) in the story to discuss what is happening. These could be:

1. Talking to her mother
2. Setting off to Granny's house
3. Seeing the wolf
4. Picking flowers
5. Arriving at Granny's house
6. What big eyes/ears/teeth you have
7. Being eaten
8. Being rescued.

On a piece of paper, ask the children to plot 'Happiness' (on the y-axis) against time (on the x-axis) for each of the points in the story. Can they mark on the graph Little Red's feeling of happiness, then see how it goes up and down. Now, on the same graph, plot the Wolf and Granny's happiness. How are they different?

Using the computers, ask the children to use a spreadsheet to plot the graphs, for example, Microsoft Excel, Apple Numbers or Google sheets. They will need to consider the scale, such as 0 to 10, or even -10 to +10 for happiness, to represent when things are going badly.

Let the children choose their own stories and create emotion graphs for them.

Teaching tip

Choose a child for each point and let them stand side-by-side, in the order they appear in the story. Trail a long piece of wool from the first child to the last. Explain that when you are happy you cheer, raising your arms up, but when you are sad you hunch downwards, lowering your arms and shoulders. Now, read the story, identifying the points. As you reach each point, ask the child to raise or lower their arms or place them somewhere in-between, depending on the mood. Now, they can see the line graph across the story, represented by the wool.

Tablet tip

Spreadsheet apps are available for tablets, such as Numbers for the iPad. If the children find it difficult to plot, they could use a simple drawing app to sketch the axes and line graph.

Understanding binary

"The children really enjoyed thinking about counting in a new way."

The old computing joke 'There are only 10 types of people who understand binary: those who do and those who don't' relates to how the binary number system works. The children really enjoy finding out about binary numbers and playing games with them.

Computers can communicate using binary code. All the data that computers send to each other is in this format. We can show the children how to count using our decimal number system, using the numbers 0, 1, 2, 3, 4, 5, 6, 7, 8 and 9, i.e. ten different digits and so named the Base10 system. With the binary number system, there are only 0 and 1, so two different digits, named Base2.

The numbers are:

In decimal	In binary
0	0
1	1
2	10
3	11
4	100
5	101
6	110
7	111
8	1000
9	1001
10	1010

In base 10, we can place the digits into columns of hundreds, tens and ones, so then number 19 could be:

100s	10s	1s
0	1	9

$(0 \times 100) + (1 \times 10) + (9 \times 1) = 19$

In binary, base 2, the columns are labelled:

16s	8s	4s	2s	1s
1	0	0	1	1

$(1 \times 16) + (0 \times 8) + (0 \times 4) + (1 \times 2) + (1 \times 1) = 19$

Ask the children to play a 'Binary fingers' game:

- Two players face each other and hold one hand behind their backs.
- They hold up between 0 and 5 fingers on the hands behind their backs.
- On the word 'Go' they show each other how many fingers they are holding up.
- The winner is the person to add up how many fingers there are in total and then say the binary number.
- For example, player 1 has 4 fingers, player 2 has 2 fingers, and so the total is 6. This translates as $(0 \times 8) + (1 \times 4) + (1 \times 2) + (0 \times 1) = 110$ in binary.

The binary digits or 'bits' can be combined when sharing information. A 'byte' is a binary code containing eight bits, for example, 01100011. It is just a way of grouping the information. Using the eight columns means that combinations of numbers up to 11111111 can be stored (this is equivalent to the number 256 in decimal). The byte is a unit of digital information. Larger numbers of bytes can be called 'megabytes', i.e. 1,000,000, bytes or 'gigabytes'.

Taking it further

Children like to hear of the terms for larger numbers and the system progresses from kilobyte, megabyte, gigabyte, terabyte, petabyte, exabyte, zettabyte to yottabyte. As technology improves so rapidly, these larger quantities of information may become more common in everyday language. An activity to introduce these larger numbers could be to display the word and the children write the number, trying to guess how many digits are needed. For example, a kilo = 1,000, mega = 1,000,000, giga = 1,000,000,000, tera = 1,000,000,000,000 (the digit 1 and 12 zeros) and yota would have the digit 1 followed by 24 zeros!

Technology around us

Part 8

Where are my chips?

"It's time to get out and about to find the technology."

The statement 'Recognise common uses of information technology beyond school' relates computing to everyday life. The children will have different experiences of technology, but many common ones, such as supermarket checkouts or phones. They need to start looking to see where computers are hiding.

Here are some ideas to get children thinking about how computers surround us every day.

- Comic strip: ask the children to bring objects to life in a comic strip, either on paper or using digital tools. They can give the object a character and show its function. Comic Life software has a free trial to try (plasq.com/downloads/comic-life-desktop).
- Animated faces: an object such as a microwave, DVD player or photocopier can tell us about its computer function using facial animation software, for example, Crazytalk (trial version available to try www.reallusion.com/crazytalk/trial.aspx). Ask the children to capture a photo of the object and animate it to describe where the computer processor may be and why it contains one. They could research technology outside of the school, for example, a vending machine or shopping till.
- Poems: ask the children to make an acrostic poem about technology. It could be using the name of the object or the word 'technology'.
- Virtual tour: using Google maps and streetview, ask the children to plan a tour to visit technology outside of school. They could locate the places where they would find the technology, then use the streetview option to zoom in and take a screenshot of each one. Then, using a presentation tool, the images can be combined to create a visual tour.

How smart is my phone?

"What makes you 'appy?"

A smart phone can run software programs called apps. What type of app would the children make, if they could design any?

Before the children make their own apps, they need to spend time looking at other apps. Start with the Apple App store or Google Play store and look at the top ten paid and free apps. Why are they popular? Do they meet a particular need? Do they sound interesting? Below each app, there is usually a review. This can show if people like it and why. Challenge the children to write a review for their favourite app.

Next the children should choose a category for the app, for example health or education. Which are the popular apps in that category and why? Encourage them to think of lots of ideas and consider who would be interested in them. App ideas are shared on Ideaswatch (www.ideaswatch.com/startup-ideas/app#) or on Pre-apps (www.preapps.com/app-ideas). They could create a Padlet.com sticky note wall to collaboratively add ideas.

In the App store, each app needs to have extra information, including:

- name
- app author's name or company
- release date
- price
- age rating.

Also, screenshots of the app need to be added. Ask the children to sketch five screens to give the impression of the app and what each screen does. Finally ask them to conduct a survey of potential users, to give them more ideas of what people would like.

Cardboard cashpoint

"Beep, beep, beep, beep, beep, kerching!"

Children will see cashpoints around the shops and in towns. They may know that people can get money out of them, but have they looked closely at them? Can they make their own cashpoint?

Show the children a video from a bank, from when cashpoints were becoming more common in the early 1990s (bit.ly/100computing75).

Cashpoints are available now to withdraw money or check the balance of an account and the children will probably have seen their parents using them. How much do they know about cashpoints? What is a PIN number? What does PIN stand for? What is a balance?

Ask the children where they have seen a cashpoint before? Have they been with their parents to get money from one? Ideally, they should visit a cash point or ask their parents to take them to see one.

What were the steps in the sequence to get some money? In groups, ask the children to create a flowchart to show the steps, for example:

1. Insert cash card
2. Enter PIN number
3. Press Enter
4. Select a service – display balance, print balance, withdraw cash, withdraw cash with receipt, other services (including change PIN or change language)
5. Remove cash card
6. Collect money
7. Remove advice slip or receipt
8. Go and spend money.

Ask the children to simulate a cash machine by role-playing the parts of the cash machine and the person using it.

Once they have created their flowchart or list of steps, ask them to create their own cashpoint using presentation software, such as PowerPoint. By placing the different screens on separate slides, they can use hyperlinks (or hyperbuttons) between slides to navigate from one to another. For example, highlight the text that says 'Check your balance' and add a hyperlink to 'Go to another slide in this presentation'. Then select the slide that has a pretend bank balance displayed as text. Don't forget to add a 'Return to main menu' link. The process of creating a non-linear presentation takes a lot of thought from the children.

Once the children have created their computer cashpoint, they can make it more real by embedding a computer into a box. Using cardboard, they can make the cashpoint surround and decorate it with the logo and name of their imaginary bank.

Tablet tip

The Tablets can make a touchscreen cashpoint possible. Using presentation software, such as Keynote, the children can add links to the slides to represent buttons. Also, they could use Scratch on the computer, or the Pyonkee app on the iPad, to program the cashpoint too!

Bonus idea ★

Ask the children to create a drinks or vending machine by showing the food and drink available and linking to the correct slide or image and asking for payment. What about making a 'fortune telling' game for the school fair? The children could press a button and it would navigate to a slide to tell their future!

SatNav

"Your destination is on the right."

Cars can have satellite navigation or 'SatNav' to tell the driver where to go. The problem is given to the SatNav of finding a place and it works out the steps needed to get there. This is an algorithm. But why is it called SatNav? Where is the satellite and how does the information travel?

Have you ever been lost? How can you find your way?

'Turn right, forwards, turn left' – the children can use instructions to direct themselves or control robots (for example the BeeBot in Idea 24). Using algorithms which follow a precise set of instructions to solve problems is very important and a good example is 'SatNav' or GPS satellite navigation for cars. Children may have seen their parents' cars use SatNav or their parents' phones giving directions. This idea not only reinforces the children's learning about algorithms, but also gets them thinking about satellites and networks.

Run the following games and activities with the children:

- Pin the tail on the donkey: the simple party game in which a blindfolded child tries to pin a tail on a picture of a donkey (the picture of a donkey, without a tail, is placed on a wall, in front of the child). This introduces the idea of giving instructions and the need for accuracy.
- Blindfold directions: where one child is blindfolded and another gives directions to move them through a maze (for example, an arrangement of tables in the classroom).
- Plotting my route: ask the children to plan their journey from home to school, using accurate instructions. To give the children

experience of other map systems, use the Ordnance Survey OpenData viewer (bit. ly/100computing76a). They can sketch a map or capture screenshots to add to a presentation. Using the Prezi presentation tool (prezi.com/) they could create a 'zooming' journey, using the maps.

- Where is the satellite? Can the children point to a satellite? Firstly, ask them if they know what a satellite is? Secondly, ask how do satellites get into space and what do they do? They may be familiar with 'Sky TV', which uses a satellite dish to get the signal. Show them a world map showing satellites and their routes (in-the-sky.org/satmap. php). Show them a 3D visualisation of the International Space Station to help them understand the view from space (bit.ly/100computing76b).
- How do SatNavs work? Ask the children to research how the satellite navigation tools work (bit.ly/100computing76c) and then explain to a partner, using a voice that sounds like a SatNav.

Try the following cross-curricular links based on SatNavs:

- English: write stories inspired by the titles 'The wrong turn' or 'The demon SatNav'.
- Maths: the children can draw large regular shapes on the school playground, following instructions.
- Science: think about rockets, satellites and geostationary orbits.
- Geography and history: look at the great explorers and make maps.
- Religious education: look at the journey to Mecca or the directions to the local church.
- Orienteering: try map reading and outdoor exercise.

Goal-line technology

"GOOOOOAAAAAAAALLLLLLLLLLLLLLLLLLLLL!"

No, it wasn't? Yes, it was! Goal-line technology has been introduced to the English Premier League. How does it know if the ball has crossed the line? Is this a good use of technology? Is it more accurate than a human?

Teaching tip

Try to find an example of technology that is of interest to your class. Do they like cats or dogs and could a sensor be used to see when they have eaten food from a bowl or returned home through a cat-flap? Could a sensor tell if a dancer had completed a move properly?

Bonus idea ★

Use videos of lessons to evaluate your own teaching or to see how the children responded to questions. For example, the VEO app (available on iTunes) from Newcastle University can enable tagging of events in the lesson. Is this a good use of technology? What could be a disadvantage of videoing lessons?

Show the children the video about goal-line technology (bit.ly/100computing77a). Now, show the video on the disallowed goal for England in the World Cup in 2010 (bit.ly/100computing77b).

Goal-line technology is an example of technology that has been introduced to football in order to reduce errors in refereeing. Different technologies have been developed to help decide if the whole of the ball has crossed the goal-line. For example, 'Hawk-Eye', which has been used in cricket and tennis, uses fast cameras to watch and predict the position of the ball. Another system, 'GoalRef' uses coils in the goal posts, which can detect a change in the magnetic field if the ball has crossed the line.

Ask the children:

- Is goal-line technology a good idea?
- What would be a reason not to use the technology? For example, do you stop the game while the referee consults the goal-line technology?
- Where else could you use this technology?

Challenge the children to design their own goal-line technology. Making a simple model and electric circuits or a MakeyMakey (Idea 42) can they simulate a goal or follow their own ideas?

AR har!

"Wow! That's amazing. Look at my picture!"

In the LEGO shop, you can hold a LEGO set box up to a camera. On a screen it will show you holding the completed model! How can we use this idea in the classroom?

Ever imagined how your LEGO set would look when it has been built? Watch the video showing LEGO augmented reality (bit.ly/100computing78a).

This is a definite 'wow' lesson. The children gasp when they first see augmented reality or AR. It is where we use real life, through a camera, and add something to it or augment it. AR involves a camera to capture the live view and a screen to display the action, with a layer of video or animation on top of it. Watch an introductory video to AR (bit.ly/100computing78b).

Look at the following examples:

- The IKEA catalogue app lets the user visualise the furniture in their own homes (bit.ly/100computing78c).
- *The Guinness World Records 2015* book has an AR app that brings its pages to life (bit.ly/100computing78d).
- The Natural History Museum has an AR dinosaur example. Visit the website (bit.ly/100computing78e) and print out the marker page (bit.ly/100computing78f). Hold the marker up to the camera to display the dinosaur on top of it on-screen.

Ask the children to create their own 3D story using 'Zooburst' (www.zooburst.com/). The books can be created and, similar to the dinosaur example, a printed code acts as the marker.

Teaching tip

So, is this helping us to learn? An art teacher explained that AR helped her children see how 3D shapes related to 2D shapes. Another teacher used an AR model of the human body, which enabled the children to see a heart working. They could rotate and interact with it, differently to if it was a video or image. If it is useful – use it!

Tablet tip

Try colAR mix, a great app, where the children can print coloured sheets and the app brings their drawings to life (colarapp.com/). Create interactive displays using the Aurasma app (www.aurasma.com/). The children can record a video of themselves describing an item, piece of artwork or writing, which is on a display board. Then, that item is used as the marker to 'trigger' playing the video. Try combining Aurasma with other apps, such as Morfo or Tellagami to add interesting videos and excite the children about their work.

Beep, beep, beep

"Everything in black and white makes sense."

Bar codes are found on items at the supermarket, but what do they do? In everyday life the children will also see the square-shaped QR (Quick Reference) codes on posters and in magazines. What are these used for and can children create their own?

At the supermarket there is a barcode on every item that is scanned at the checkout. Not only can the shopper see how much an item costs, the bill can be calculated and charged, the receipt printed and the stock can be controlled. As the item is sold, the supermarket knows when to re-order more. It will inform them which items are most popular or more popular at different times of the year. All this information is held in the bar code.

The children may also have seen QR codes. These are square black and white patterns (www.whatisaqrcode.co.uk). QR codes are similar to the black and white striped ones, but can contain more information (they can be called 2D barcodes, as they can hold information along the x-axis and y-axis). In school, we can link display work to a website. Using a QR code reader app on a tablet or mobile phone, the user can point the camera at the QR code and then view the website straight away (without having to type in the long web address).

Get children to record a video (for example, a short explanation of a QR code) and upload it to a website, such as Vimeo or YouTube. Using a QR code they could link to it and view it immediately. To create a QR code, the website QR stuff allows the text or web address to be added. The longer the text, the more complicated the pattern will be (www.qrstuff.com/).

Robots rule!

"Can machines think?"

Robots can be found working in factories or cleaning floors in houses. If you could have a robot, what would it do? Could they take over the world?

The Turing test is a test of a machine's ability to exhibit intelligent behaviour equivalent to, or indistinguishable from, that of a human. Alan Turing introduced the test in his 1950 paper 'Computing Machinery and Intelligence', which began with the words: 'I propose to consider the question, "Can machines think?"'

Get the children to use Edward de Bono's Thinking Hats strategy to discuss 'Can machines think?' (bit.ly/100computing80). Consider a different aspect of the question for each hat:

- white hat – information: state the facts, without opinion
- yellow hat – positives: reasons why machines can think
- black hat – negatives: reasons why machines cannot think
- red hat – feelings and emotions: how the children feel about their opinion
- green hat – creativity and alternatives: explore new ideas about `what if machines could think or not'
- blue hat – thinking process: the metacognition about the whole process.

Using the Thinking Hats strategy takes practice and the children may need the teacher to guide each step of the process by using prompting questions, but without influencing the children's thinking. If the children had their own robot, what would it be able to do? Would it pass the Turing test?

Teaching tip

Using the Six Thinking Hats process is a great way for the children to consider different points of view. The children will need to try the process several times to use it effectively. Visual clues of real hats or pictures of the coloured hats, with keywords, can help them remember which hat they are discussing and what it represents.

Taking it further

Alan Turing is considered to be one of the pioneers of computer science (www.bbc.co.uk/history/people/alan_turing). He was instrumental in deciphering codes during the Second World War and was influential in the development of computers.

Back to the future

"Roads? Where we're going, we don't need roads!"

What will technology look like in 30 years time? It's time for some 'crystal ball gazing' — what can the children imagine?

My son was two years old when the first iPad was released. Even though there had been other tablets before, this seemed like a big move forward with the technology. For my son, they have always been around. I showed him a floppy disk and had to explain what it was — I suppose he has only ever seen one as the 'Save' icon on a word processor.

Technology is moving forwards all the time and what we may think is advanced today will seem old and basic in the future.

Ray Kurzweil is an inventor and futurist (www.kurzweilai.net/ray-kurzweil-biography). He has joined Google to help them develop human interaction with searching the web. He has given interesting talks about technology and the future, including one of his TED talks (www.ted.com/talks/ray_kurzweil_on_how_technology_will_transform_us). Watch the talk and transcribe the ideas for the children or even let the children watch it and see what they make of it. Let the children think that their job title is 'futurist' — what do they imagine that role would involve?

The film *Back to the future part II* is set in the year 2015. It has hover boards, flying cars and self-adjusting clothing. Show excerpts to inspire the children to think about the future and the possibilities. Can they produce a poster or a cardboard prototype for their future product? These can be really fun ideas, where the children can imagine anything!

It's time to go back to the future!

Progression

Part 9

What do you want to know?

"Want a quick way to find out what the children know? Even better, want to find out what they want to learn next?"

We can brainstorm to find out what the children know at the start of a topic, but do we ever ask them what they would want to know?

Give each child a sticky note, and ask them to add an idea and place it on the wall. You can then step back and look at the responses. At the start of a topic, you could ask them to write down everything they already know, for example, about networks. At the end of the lesson, week or topic, you could ask again and see which facts or ideas they have learned about. Using sticky notes is one way of gathering their ideas, but you can also use online, digital notes.

Using Padlet (padlet.com) to set up an online wall (set up a free account, then all of the walls you create will be listed). By sharing the web address of the wall, you can add digital sticky notes, collaboratively and at the same time. You can revisit the wall it in your next lesson or even several months later.

Once the children have added their ideas to the wall, you can drag them to the left-hand side. This is what they know. Now ask, 'What do you want to know?' Place new notes in the middle of the wall and use them as a stimulus for planning your upcoming lessons.

When the topic is complete, return to the wall and get children to add a note about something they have learned. This is our KWL wall:

What do you KNOW?
What do you WANT to know?
What have you LEARNED?

PechaKucha

"20 slides? 20 seconds each? Now, there's a challenge!"

PechaKucha is a style of presenting 20 images, each one for 20 seconds. No more boring presentations!

In a PechaKucha style presentation each of the 20 images will automatically display for 20 seconds, before moving on to the next one. This keeps the momentum going and creates an exciting presentation. It was invented by Astrid Klein and Mark Dytham in 2003, as a way of presenting information about architecture. It meant that it would limit the presenters to 20 images and, as they are images without text, the presenter needed to think about what they were going to say and not read out the words.

Try using this technique with the children:

- A 20-slide presentation lasts for nearly seven minutes, which may be a little daunting. Instead, try reducing it to five slides, changing every 20 seconds. Obviously, you can adapt the format for different ages or abilities.
- The children could do a short presentation about their lives, growing up or about a hobby. By choosing something familiar, it will help them try out the format. They need to think about the words they will use and to script the words for each image. They will also need to rehearse to practise the timings.
- Once the children have presented something familiar, using this PechaKucha format, they could use it to show their progress with their work. They can take screenshots each week over their computing projects, so they have the images. They can then talk about their progression from week to week.

Teaching tip

When asking the children to present, encourage them to plan out their words using a simple table. They may be saying approximately three words per second, so if they draft their words for a 20-second slide, they will need around 50–60 words as a maximum. If they have a few less, then they can pause at the start and end of each slide.

Tablet tip

Using an app, such as Shadow Puppet Edu, the children can add images and a narration over the top of them. It helps them to construct the video and also lets them practise their narration and re-record it. Some children will find it easier to prepare a video of their images, with narration, rather than standing up and presenting live.

Send a problem

"Why not ask someone in your class? I'm sure they have good ideas!"

What's your biggest problem? Has anyone got any ideas to help? What will you do next? Show the children how to use large envelopes to 'send' their problems to get new ideas to solve them.

Teaching tip

It may work better if children work in small groups to discuss and come up with the problem to solve. Then, when the envelopes are passed around, there are fewer turns before they return to their owners. As the envelope moves on to each child, they should discuss their ideas, before adding one to the envelope. A large visual timer is useful, so the class can see how long they have, or use a piece of music and when that song ends, it is time to pass the envelopes.

Tablet tip

Using a mind-mapping tool, such as Popplet, the children could add an idea or branch to the central problem. So, the tablet could be passed around the room and each group adds an addition branch or, if it is related to another suggestion, join their idea to that one.

One of the ways I've seen the children develop is by encouraging them to be able to identify their own problems. They need to think carefully about a problem they need to solve and how to put it into words. Tell the children that they can 'send a problem' to get help:

- Ask them to write their problem in the middle of a large envelope. For example, 'I'm making an app for a children's charity. What features should it have?' or 'My computer program is not working. What should I do first to fix it?'
- The envelopes are then passed clockwise around the class to the next pupil. They have three minutes to read the problem and add an idea of how to solve it, by writing on the envelope. Then the envelopes are passed and the three minutes begin again. It is important to keep to time, so that they do not rush to add an answer, but to also have thinking time before writing.
- Once the envelopes have been around the class, they should be returned to the original owner. Now they have lots of new ideas, and the children have also been reading these suggestions as the envelopes were passed.
- After reading all the suggestions on the envelope, the children need to decide if they are going to follow the advice or explain if it has helped them create a new solution.
- At the end of the lesson, week or topic, the children can summarise on the back of the envelope what they did and how the advice of 'sending a problem' helped them.

Peer pupil progress

"Wow, look at your computer program, it's brilliant!"

By observing each other, the children learn about how their friends approach problems and they will learn about themselves too.

Children will know who is the best footballer in the class. They can also probably tell you which pupils are the best artists, dancers or musicians. What about with their computing work? How could they decide what is 'good' work and how can they describe it? To get the children thinking, play a game of 'Mirrors':

- In groups of three, decide who will be numbers one, two and three. The number one child moves about and number two needs to try to copy their poses. This could be done to music, where they freeze positions when the music stops.
- Once they have frozen their pose, number three looks at number two and decides how well they have copied number one. They might use words such as same, opposite, lower, higher, identical, different.
- Now swap, so that number one observes, number two moves and number three copies. Then finally, swap places again.
- This activity should help them to see how the observer needs to evaluate the work and use words which they can all understand.

Now, the same three children will assess their own work (either a written piece or on the computer). Each of them presents their own example and compares it with their peers' examples. Can they spot where there are similarities or differences? Can they explain in simple words, why one person's work is better than the other? Can they see where they have improved their work, showing progress?

Teaching tip

On a PC, the 'PrintScreen' can save a screenshot into the computer's Clipboard and then paste it into another program, for example, Microsoft PowerPoint. On a Mac, the 'cmd' and 'Shift' and '3' takes a whole screenshot, or by using 'cmd' and 'Shift' and '4', an area of the screen can be captured. The children can annotate their work in many ways. They could print their screen shot and write over it in pen or add sticky notes. They could use software, such as Skitch (available for PC, Mac, iPad, Android), which enables them to add arrows, labels and shapes to an image. Using screenshots may help the children compare the work.

Tablet tip

To capture a screenshot on an iPad, press the 'Screen lock' button and the 'Home' button at the same time. On an Android tablet, press the 'Power' and 'Volume down' buttons together.

Trails and tracking

"What did you do at school today?"

Ask a child what they did at school that day and it can be difficult to find out. By using digital tools, we can look at child's history and track their progress.

If you ask children, 'What did you do in the last lesson?', they can often forget or find it hard to explain. Even in a lesson, if you were to ask them to describe the changes or improvements they have added to their work, it may be a struggle. Use digital tools to support you:

- In software such as Microsoft Word, PowerPoint or Google Docs you can add comments. Comments are really useful and reflect how real programmers work. They may add a comment in a program to explain to themselves or others what they have done or how that piece of code works. In Word, there is the 'Review' menu, where a new yellow, sticky note comment can be added. This is similar in Google Docs. When you collaborate on a document or presentation online (Goggle Docs or Microsoft 365) real-time commenting can take place.
- The 'Version history' tool in Google Docs displays the previous versions of a document so you can view the changes over time.
- Get children to get create a presentation using screenshots (see Idea 11), and a date and time, so they can show their progress.
- 'Track changes' can be used where a document is shared with another person, maybe for review. The tool will keep a record of the changes that are made to the document, with a date and time stamp. Therefore, a child can share a document with their peers or you and the comments and changes made can be recorded.

Sticky note parents

"Getting parental feedback can be hard to do."

Involving parents is important, but it can be hard to get their feedback. Using online sticky notes is one good way to gather comments, especially when the parent is interviewed by the child.

Padlet is a very versatile tool. You can set up a communal wall for notes to be added in a 'free form' way. As Padlet is online, the notes can be added from anywhere in the world. A school in England, for example, collaborated with a school in Canada on a joint project. It was similar to pen friends, but the updates happened every day. The children were comfortable adding notes and could do so from a PC, Mac, tablet or phone.

Parents might need help from the children to prompt them and then to actually add the note. Once the children are familiar with Padlet, ask them to interview their parents to gain one idea for feedback. Once interviewed, the children can help their parents add the note. If necessary, check the 'Moderate comments' box in the 'Privacy' settings for the wall so that the wall owner can approve notes before they go live. This is good for control, though it means that the teacher has to check the notes, and they will not appear instantly. The layout of the notes can be changed, using the 'Layout' options, in the settings:

- 'Free form' allows notes to go anywhere
- 'Stream' places the notes in a stack, showing one after the other
- 'Grid' organises the notes, so they do not overlap.

The parental feedback wall can be exported as an image or PDF, to keep as evidence. The wall can be used to respond to the parents, adding new comments in reply to their notes.

Teaching tip

When using Padlet, the page may need to be refreshed to display the notes. The browser page can be reloaded and the new notes should appear. When using the moderation mode in a lesson, it may be possible to use one or two pupils as the moderators. They can decide why they think comments should be allowed or not, developing their evaluation and communication skills.

Tablet tip

Other sticky note tools are available, such as the Lino-it app. These can have different features or provide a different experience for collaboration. It is good to show the children a range of tools and allow them to select the appropriate one for the task.

Video games homework

"What's your high score?"

In video games, there are many achievements which encourage the children to complete a level and progress to the next one. How could we use this in our lessons?

Video games have evolved, becoming more and more complex, but also including more ways to celebrate achievement. On the Xbox, the player can be given achievements for completing parts of a game, which are then kept and displayed in their Xbox records as badges.

Ask the children to name and describe their progress through a video game. What are the main steps, achievements and rewards? If they do not play video games, ask them to think about a sport, such as swimming or gymnastics. Ask them what they would give achievements for in school. How could they spot their own progress, reward it and share with others?

Working in groups, let the children think of a badge they would give in their lessons, for example, a 'Working scientifically' badge. What would it look like? What are the criteria to earn one? What would be the next badge? Do the badges join to form a 'Super badge'? Ask the children to design their badges and then prepare a presentation to share with the class. They could list their features under the headings:

- Name of badge
- Subject area
- Criteria to earn the badge
- Next badge to earn.

Ask them to create the designs, either on paper or on computers. How would they display their badges? Would a classroom display or booklet work? Would they want an online method to share with the world?

Time to pack up!

"Packing up at the end of the lesson is valuable evaluation time."

Can we use tidying up for assessment? Do the children have a routine for saving or sharing their work?

Use the following ideas to help the children become more aware of the packing-up period:

- Display a timer with a countdown so the children can see how long is remaining. There are several timers available online, including ipadstopwatch.com (which allows custom countdowns to be created).
- Try playing music so the children can hear how long is remaining. They could, for example, save their work and tidy up by the end of the song (the progress through the song is displayed on the music player). Try 'The Final Countdown' by Europe or other time-related songs.
- Try using a video timer, which can help to engage the children (for example, bit.ly/100computing89). As with all YouTube or video content, check before the lesson to ensure the videos are appropriate.
- Using the Google search, try typing '1 minute timer' into the search box. It should display a countdown on the search results page.

How can we use the packing-up part of the lesson to show progress and get the children to identify what they have done? One idea is to use drywipe boards. Once each child has finished packing up (by the end of the timer) they could write on their board one thing they have learnt or done differently that lesson, then hold it up. You can not only see who is ready, but also see their thoughts. This can then feed into the plenary session or inform the planning for the next lesson.

Teaching tip

If drywipe boards are not available, DVD cases with white card inside can make small boards to use. The children could write using a drywipe pen on the outside or write on paper and place it inside the DVD case cover, for display.

Tablet tip

Using an app such as Big Text Free allows the user to enter text and display it in large text on the screen. Alternatively, a word-processing app with a large font would display their learning across the screen for the teacher to see.

Showing progress

"When being observed, make sure you can show where the children are and where they are going."

When working with teachers, I've been asked if they should do 'mini-plenaries' with the class if an observer walks in. My advice is only do a mini-plenary if it is helping the children's understanding. So, how else can you show they are making progress, so that others can see too?

If an observer walks in at the beginning of the lesson, it can be easier for them to see what the children are learning and how they are going to do it. However, if they arrive during the lesson, how can the learning and progress be emphasised? A short plenary could review the learning so far and show what they have understood, but if it is going to stop the children unnecessarily then it is not a good use of their time.

A traffic light system may help:

- If the children are working on the computers, give them three cards: red, amber and green. Say 'Traffic lights' and they should place one of the cards on their computer screen (using sticky tack).
- By looking around the room, you can see who thinks they know what they are doing and are getting on with it (green). Those displaying amber may just need a small bit of help to clarify the learning so they can then keep going. Those with the red cards could be brought together at the front of the class to explain what to do.
- Alternatively, the amber cards could first ask a green card pupil, before asking you. If there are too many amber cards, then it may be worth saying ambers ask a green and then in five minutes display the traffic lights again, to see if they have understood.

- The traffic lights idea aims to quickly assess if the children are able to understand what they are doing. At the same time as you say 'Traffic lights', the children could take a screenshot, as evidence of progress in the lesson.

Digital survey tools, such as Socrative.com, can really help to display progress. If the children log into the teacher's Socrative room at the start of the lesson, then periodically (or when the observer arrives) you can ask a question. For example, a quick survey question like the traffic lights could be asked, 'Answer A if you know what to do or E if you do not or BCD if you are unsure'. Also, a question based on the lesson objectives could be asked at the beginning of the lesson and a new one during it, for example, 'Everyone answer the question, what should you do if you see an image which upsets you? Choose from answers ABC.' This should not interrupt their work too much, but give you and the observer a snapshot of their learning and progress, as the answers are displayed on the classroom screen.

Taking it further

Screenshots are a way of capturing a picture of the entire computer or tablet screen. Early in a lesson, the children can take a screenshot and also another one towards the end, as evidence of their progress. They can add the images to a presentation and add annotations to explain how they have progressed during the lesson.

Bonus idea ★

Another tablet tool is called 'Plickers' (plickers.com). This could be used to get feedback on the children's opinion of their progress. Each child has a card, with a unique square pattern on it. Written in small text is the number of the card and also the letters 'A, B, C and D' around the four sides of the square. The teacher can ask a question and give up to four possible answers. The children give an answer by holding up the card (with their choice of letter to the top). Using the tablet, it scans the cards and records the answers. Therefore, the teacher can collect information about the class and the children can give their answers, without telling their peers.

Assessment

Part 10

The Three Little Pigs

"Straw, sticks and bricks – three things to show how you've improved."

In the traditional story of *The Three Little Pigs*, there are three materials tested: straw, sticks, bricks. Can the children see three points in their work where they have improved?

Ask the children to look at their work. Is there something that they have changed? Did it improve each time? Did they need to try something else to make it better?

Ask the children to fold paper books to make a record of their work (see bit.ly/foldapaperbook). On each double-page spread, ask them to identify, for example, the part of the program, image or wording they have changed. Then they can say how it has improved the work.

- Peer-review is then a good way forward: children explain how they have changed their work to a partner, who gives them feedback. They could feed back to explain how well the work has improved or give further ideas of what to do next.
- By identifying the piece of work, drawing on paper and explaining it verbally, the children will think about their improvements at least three times. This helps them to embed the learning and also to think about the persuasive language they can use in explaining their improvements.

Some children may need direction to identify an area of their work they have improved. Try displaying prompts of areas to look for:

- Have you made your instructions clearer?
- Have you made your program more efficient (not using the same lines many times)?
- Can another person understand what to do more quickly?

Tablet tip

There are tablet apps that allow books to be made, for example, Book Creator is an excellent tool. A template book could be created, with simple instructions for the children to complete inside. Also, some children may enjoy recording their voices to explain their improvements.

Road mapping the learning

"SLOW Children ahead"

Some signs we see do not make sense or can have a double meaning. We can evaluate the signs to see if their meaning is clear. If the children were to make their own signs or symbols for their learning, what would they look like?

Show the children examples of the UK road signs. Can they guess what they mean? Can they recognise that different shapes and colours have meaning? Is their meaning clear? Get children to think about how they could signpost their own learning, as well as their friends' learning:

- In the classroom ask the children what signs they think should be on the walls. Perhaps 'Learning ahead' on the door? Get them to design the signs, using the computers or tablets. Once complete, ask them to show their signs to other groups and see if the meaning is clear.
- Encourage the children to design signs for feedback about their own work. It could, for example, be a triangular warning sign if they have not understood completely or a blue motorway-style sign if they have made fast progress. They could have 'Stop' and 'Go' signs for when they need to see you or to continue with their work.
- Give a project a road map, to explain where it is heading, including 'milestones' to indicate progress. Challenge the children to 'road map' their learning. They could begin by mapping their progress earlier in the year. The milestones would be the important events that have occurred. Next, in groups, ask them to think about the next 30, 60 and 90 days (or by half term, Christmas, Easter or end of the year). Where do they want to be?

Collaborating on concepts

"Working together face-to-face and using online tools can be a powerful combination."

When we work together, in the same room, we listen to each other, watch each other and collaborate. Online tools enable collaboration too, which could be remotely accessed. By combining the online tools with face-to-face collaboration, we can work together, on the same page!

When working online, we probably won't be able to see each other. Even when using video to communicate, it can be difficult to see facial expressions. The children need to consider how it can be different when working face-to-face and online. Try the following ideas:

- When working in groups, there can be problems, such as certain children dominating the conversation or not allowing others to speak. In pairs, ask one child to tell a story while the other keeps interrupting. Do their faces show their feelings?
- How about if we cannot see each other? Try the exercise again with the children sitting back to back. Challenge them to tell the story in an angry, happy or sad voice. Can their partner guess their mood?
- Using paper sticky notes, ask the children to think of a familiar story. Can they think of facts about that story? Write each fact on a sticky note and post them on the wall.
- Select two children to organise the notes into groups, with advice from others.
- Observe how they work together. Do they take turns? Do they watch each other to see what they are doing? Does one dominate? Compare this to if the children were working together online. They need to take turns, watch and listen to the other people online, if they want to communicate clearly.

Teaching tip

When working with the class, set up a whiteboard for each group. On your web browser, open a new tab for each whiteboard, so that you can follow what is happening, in real time.

Tablet tip

The online sticky note tool 'Padlet' could be used to recreate the sticky note activity above (padlet. com). Another online tool for collaboration is Conceptboard (conceptboard.com/) which enables people to write on same whiteboard. Images can be uploaded, discussed and annotated. Try it out with the class and see how it could work. Do they listen to each other and collaborate to share ideas? Do they find it easier to collaborate when in the same room compared to being online?

Giving feed-quack

"The children loved making paper ducks, then they had to choose words to evaluate each other's work."

Giving the children a common language for giving feedback helps them to explain their thoughts more clearly to their peers. Help them to establish the important points to make and then decide on a list of helpful words. Then they can give feedback to their friends with more clarity.

Teaching tip

If the groups look too unfair in the early rounds, for example, one group is not very good at folding ducks, try having a transfer window, where they can sacrifice points, to buy in someone from another group. This can either mix up the groups or make them more determined to make better ducks.

When the children are describing their work and how well they have completed it, they often struggle to find the right words. Sometimes the words they use are not familiar and they can misunderstand each other. There have been many times I've given feedback in my marking only to discover that the child has not understood what I meant. So, we need a strategy to develop our common language.

Folding paper into ducks may not seem like an assessment activity, but actually, the children are developing their vocabulary as they follow the instructions. Example instructions can be found online (www.wikihow.com/Fold-an-Origami-Duck).

Introduce a time limit to make the activity more competitive, as the children have to balance quantity with quality. Once the children have learned how to fold the ducks, then the games can begin. Ideally, they will use coloured paper of four different colours. If this is not available, you could modify the rules.

Begin the game by placing the children into groups of four. Then explain that they are in charge of a duck-making factory. Using a timer, set for five minutes, give them the first task:

- make as many ducks as possible in five minutes.

When the time is up, ask them to look at the ducks. Which team made the most ducks? Can each group organise their ducks in order from the best to worst? What were the criteria they used to evaluate the ducks? Neat folds? Symmetrical? No unwanted creases? One of the group should write the shared words as a list.

The second task is:

- make as many ducks as possible that are high quality, in one minute.

This time, they should take more care to create better quality ducks. Choose one person from each team to be the 'Quality control' person. They should visit another team and remove any 'low-quality' ducks, with explanations. Now, which team made the most high-quality ducks? Keep a running score for each group.

The third task could be:

- make as many as possible, in five minutes, that are a pretty colour.

When they have finished, choose one child to state which colour was pretty. For example, if they choose light blue, then each team should discard any ducks that are not that colour. They should say that this is unfair and if they had known the colour to begin with, they would have used that colour. Repeat this again, choosing a different child to pick a colour.

Finally, choose a colour (for example, yellow) and then set this task:

- make as many ducks as possible, in one minute, that are yellow and high quality.

This time they should find it easier to get a high score. They know what is expected of them and they have developed an understanding of the words used to evaluate the ducks.

Clearly make the link between setting up an activity, where they need to understand what is required, and evaluating and marking, where they need to know what makes a high-quality outcome.

Tablet tip

The children could use the camera on a tablet to keep a record of their high-quality ducks. They could use Skitch to label the features that make it a better duck. Another app is 'Shadow Puppet Edu', which allows the children to place photos in order and add a narration. They could take photos of the paper ducks, at each stage of their folding, place them in order and record their voices explaining how to create the paper ducks.

Bonus idea ★

Create a glossary of words for giving feedback. For each word, display it on the classroom wall and ask the children to describe how they might use it in a sentence. Do the other children think the word has been used appropriately?

Habits of mind

"What do you do when you don't know what to do?"

'Habits of Mind' is knowing how to behave intelligently, when you do not know what to do. You may have a problem and cannot think how to begin to solve it. The sixteen habits can help to show how the children can approach problems.

A few years ago, I was working on a game-based learning project, using Nintendo Wii consoles. We could see that the children could persist with their problem-solving, helping and advising each other, explaining why they did something, showing how they had understood the challenges and trying to get a high score by being more accurate. We were looking for a way of expressing this when I was introduced to the 'Habits of Mind'. These are sixteen ways to behave intelligently when faced with a new situation. This seemed to fit perfectly with the children and they began to unpick what each statement meant to them.

The 16 Habits of Mind were developed by Arthur Costa and Bena Kallick and they are:

- Persisting
- Thinking and communicating with clarity and precision
- Managing impulsivity
- Gathering data through all senses
- Listening with understanding and empathy
- Creating, imagining, innovating
- Thinking flexibly
- Responding with wonderment and awe
- Thinking about thinking (metacognition)
- Taking responsible risks
- Striving for accuracy
- Finding humour
- Questioning and posing problems
- Thinking interdependently

- Applying past knowledge to new situations
- Remaining open to continuous learning

No single habit has a priority over the others. Also, when considering a problem or new situation, you do not need to use all or even most of them. They are simply sixteen ways to behave when you don't know what to do.

Some of the statements are easier to understand. 'Persisting' with a problem would mean the children would stick at a problem to try to solve it. 'Striving for accuracy' would mean trying to make the solution as accurate as they can. However, what does 'Thinking interdependently' mean? Working with the children, they explained it as relying on each other's thinking, so one person's thoughts help another.

When looking at the list, there are many statements which we would like to see happening in our lessons. They fit well with computing, for example, where we want the children to be more precise, accurate, take responsible risks, ask questions and use previous knowledge.

As a first step introduce the statements to the children and try to show where they have used them. Then you can see if they can identify where they might use them in their work.

A classroom display is a great way of reinforcing the Habits and also using symbols to represent each one. Ask the children to design symbols for the Habits or take photographs to show them in action.

The Habits of Mind were first published as a series of books (Costa, A and Kallick, B (2000) *Habits of Mind: A Developmental Series* Alexandria, VA: Association for Supervision and Curriculum Development).

SOLO

"The SOLO Taxonomy gives the children a way of showing their understanding."

The SOLO Taxonomy (Structure of Observed Learning Outcomes) gives us a shared vocabulary to explain our understanding of our work. The children can look at the five stages and say why they are at a particular one.

When I was introduced to the SOLO Taxonomy, I was enthused by forward-thinking teachers Darren Mead, Chris Harte, John Sayers, Martin Said and Zoe Elder. They showed how they have used the SOLO taxonomy in their lessons and I wanted to find out more. It was developed by John Biggs and Kevin Collis in 1982, to describe the five stages children move through in their learning. It is described by Pam Hook as: 'What am I learning? How is it going? What do I do next?'

The five stages of the SOLO taxonomy are:

- Prestructural - the children have bits of knowledge, which are not organised.
- Unistructural – simple connections are made between the bits of knowledge, but they are not sure why they are significant.
- Multistructural – connections between the bits of knowledge are made, but they are not sure of the bigger picture.
- Relational – the children can connect the bits of knowledge and understand how they fit into the bigger picture.
- Extended abstract – the children have made lots of connections between the bits of knowledge and they can generalise their learning, to apply it in another problem or subject.

The children can self-identify where they are in their learning, using this common framework.

For example, if they are learning about being safe online, they may know that Facebook is a way to connect online and that they can communicate with others. They would be starting to connect the bits of knowledge, but not realise the significance (Unistructural). If they began to realise that social media was a way for people to communicate, that they could contact 'friends' on Facebook, but these may be people they have not met face-to-face and that they need to be careful when online to report if someone makes them feel uncomfortable, then they are moving from Multistructural to Relational, understanding the bigger picture of e-safety. For more on Facebook, see Idea 50.

Another example could be programming using the Scratch software. Before the children have used Scratch, they are Prestructual. When they have made simple programs to move a character forwards, across the screen or to change the look of the character, they are Unistructural. Once they begin to create more complex programs, using 'repeat' and 'if . . . then . . . else' statements, then they may be Multistructural. When they are thinking carefully about their programs, understanding how the Scratch commands work together to solve the problem, the children may be working at a Relational level. To take their learning and apply it to a new problem and program would be Extended Abstract. The children can begin to see where they are in their learning about programming.

Further reading can be found on Pam Hook's website (pamhook.com/solo-taxonomy/). It will take time to introduce the children to the new vocabulary and to start to recognise where they are in their learning. However, this investment in time will be repaid, as they are able to see where they are and what they need to do next.

(Biggs J and Collis K (1982) *Evaluating the Quality of Learning: the SOLO taxonomy* New York: Academic Press)

Taking it further

The SOLO Taxonomy is not just for working with the children. Why not organise the staff professional development using it? The teachers in your school will be at different stages in their learning, for example, when using tablet computers. By using the SOLO method, more effective learning can take place.

Which is the best answer?

"Often, I will ask a question and then listen to a pupil's answer, but should I ask others what they think of the answer?"

When we ask a question of a pupil, they will give an answer, but often we will then ask another pupil another question. Perhaps instead we should ask another pupil to evaluate the answer and see if they can improve it.

In whole-class discussions we ask many questions. Often, however, we are so busy thinking about the next question or what we are going to do next, that we do not pause to really evaluate the pupils' answers.

One approach is to ask the question, wait for the children to think about it, and choose three children to respond. As a class you can then all listen to their responses and decide which answer was the best. The children could vote by raising their hands. Ask one person from each group of voters to explain why they think is it a good answer. You can ask how the answers could be improved too.

The Google job application questions do not have a definitive answer; they are more about the person's approach to answering them:

- How many tennis balls can fit in a school?
- How much should you charge to wash all the cars in your street?
- Why are satellite dishes round?

Display one of the Google job-style questions for the class to view. Let them look at the question and think. Let three children share their answers and then let the class vote on their preferred answer. Ask a child to evaluate their chosen answer, by explaining why they chose it. Could the answer be improved? Finally, do you think the child who answered would get the job at Google?

Reframing the question

"Let me ask you that question in another way."

How else could you ask a question? Can you draw it or choose a picture to help explain what you mean? Working in pairs is especially important to develop listening skills and then speaking skills to reframe the question.

In the game Pictionary one player selects a card and draws whatever is named on it, and the other players have to guess what it is. The players need to look at the drawing and ask questions, while the drawer has to listen and then clarify the drawing. They are reframing their drawing to make it clearer.

Try playing a game of Pictionary with the class. Divide them into two teams, select a mixture of films, TV programmes or computing words and let them draw them on the board.

When we ask a question in lessons, we sometimes need to reframe it. When we reframe a picture, it is taken from one frame and placed into another. Reframing questions is when we place the question in another context or change the words, to help the person understand what we are asking. In pairs, ask the children to ask each other a question. Encourage them to listen carefully. They should then repeat back to their partner what they think they are asking. The first person then asks the same question in a slightly different way, to clarify their partner's response. The partner then tries to answer the question. So, the steps are: ask; repeat back; ask again; reply. The children could also draw the question, the partner could draw a reply and then they could clarify, before an answer is drawn. The type of questions could be: How does a computer connect to the Internet? Why would a person bully another person online? What is a loop in a program?

Teaching tip

The questions could be differentiated using Bloom's Revised Taxonomy – Remember, Understand, Apply, Create, Synthesise, Evaluate. For example, simpler questions could be: How many . . . ? Who was it that . . . ? What is . . . ?

More complex questions could be: Can you define . . . ? If this happened, then what would be the effect on . . . ? Is there a better answer to . . . ?

Tablet tip

The children can draw on the tablet, using simple tools such as Doodle Buddie. The Explain Everything app can allow the drawings and conversations to be recorded as evidence.

3-2-1 action

"Don't point the camera at me, it adds an extra chin and you can see up my nose!"

Some children are happy to appear on camera and some are not. By filming a piece of work while talking about it, they can explain their learning and we can capture assessment evidence.

A new word to enter the *Oxford English Dictionary* is 'selfie' – taking a picture of yourself, often in an interesting place. We sometimes do not want to appear on camera, but the selfie craze has made this popular.

We can use video to record our thoughts. Some programmes, such as Big Brother, include a chair in which participants sit to give reflections on events and their feelings. Photos and videos can be captured easily using webcams, cameras and tablet computers.

Some children may be happy to speak to the camera, to give their feedback on an activity or piece of work. This piece of video is great evidence of their learning, for example, if they describe how their team worked together to solve a problem. However, some children may not want to appear in a video. How can we capture their understanding? Try these ideas:

- Instead of pointing the camera at the child, let them point the camera at their piece of work. If they have written a program, they could hold the camera up to the screen to record the video, while speaking into the microphone. This way, we can still record their voice and see their work.
- When children have solved a problem using the BeeBot robot, they can show the BeeBot in action while narrating. If they have more than one video of the process of solving the problem, we can see their progression.

Open badges

"Badges for skills, badges for achievement, badges for teamwork – what would you give a badge for?"

In organisations such as the Scouts or Girl Guides, badges are given for particular skills or experiences. Badges can also recognise 'soft skills' like teamwork or communication. Digital badges are becoming popular now too.

Open Badges (openbadges.org) is a concept from Mozilla that is designed to recognise achievement, whether it is a particular skill, such as making a web page, or taking part in running an event to teach others. Because it is a digital badge it can be displayed anywhere and linked to evidence, for example, a video of the person taking part in an event.

Anyone can create a digital badge, but the recognition comes with the endorsements. If it was a badge offered by your school, then you would be endorsing it. If you could get another school or a local business to endorse it too, that adds weight to it. If you have larger organisations like Google or Mozilla behind it, then that gives it even greater credence.

A UK company that has developed digital badges is Digital Me (www.digitalme.co.uk/badges). They began with the Supporter to Reporter programme, which encouraged children to report upon sports events. They then developed the Badge the UK programme (www.digitalme.co.uk/badgetheuk), to support people to create, issue and endorse badges.

Could you offer a digital badge? What would it be for? Can the children decide? How can you share their badges? Put the badges on to a blog and get the children writing about how they achieved it. Could you get local businesses or charities involved to endorse the badges?

Teaching tip

Holding a badge-making workshop is a great way to engage the children. They can use card, pens and glue to make a physical badge. They can describe what it is for and how to achieve it. The time making the physical badges allows for lots of conversation. They can then convert the physical to digital, by recreating the badge on the computer, for sharing.

Tablet tip

The app Credly is an example of a digital badge maker. The children can create badges and issue them to each other. This could be a 'Best friend' badge or a 'Teamwork' badge, but they must think about the criteria to earn the badges too.

Glossary

Algorithms: A series of instructions, to solve a problem.

Data: Numbers sent from one computer to another. The data can represent text, images, videos, sound, for example.

Debug: To remove mistakes from a program.

Decomposition: Breaking a bigger problem into smaller parts, which can then be solved.

Evaluation: Looking at the solution to a problem and seeing how well it solves it.

Generalisation: Taking the learning or pattern from one solution and using it somewhere else.

Input: Putting information into a computer. An input device could be a mouse, keyboard or touchscreen, for example.

Internet: Computer networks that are connected together, from all around the world. They communicate using the same protocols (TCP/IP).

Network: A computer network is where computers are joined together, so they can communicate with each other.

Output: Getting information out of a computer. An output device could be a screen, printer or speakers, for example.

Program: The precise set of instructions, which can be carried out by a computer.

Protocols: Ways of communicating together. One computer sends data and another computer can understand it, because it is organised in a way they both understand.

Selection: IF something happens THEN do this ELSE do that.

Software: The programs that work on a computer to carry out the precise instructions.

Subroutines or Procedures: Parts of a program, which may be used more than once, to make the program more efficient.

Variables: How data can be stored in a program. For example, in a game - the number of lives, the score, the time.

Web search: To find data on the World Wide Web, based on keywords.

World Wide Web: The information shared across the internet, around the world. The web pages are written in hypertext, which includes web links to other pages.